Photo by Captain Edward Steichen

Faces of War

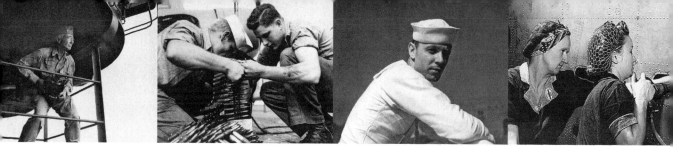

Faces of War

THE UNTOLD STORY OF EDWARD STEICHEN'S
WWII PHOTOGRAPHERS

★　　★　　★

Mark D. Faram

BERKLEY CALIBER
NEW YORK

THE BERKLEY PUBLISHING GROUP
Published by the Penguin Group
Penguin Group (USA) Inc.
375 Hudson Street, New York, New York 10014, USA
Penguin Group (Canada), 90 Eglinton Avenue East, Suite 700, Toronto, Ontario M4P 2Y3, Canada
(a division of Pearson Penguin Canada Inc.)
Penguin Books Ltd., 80 Strand, London WC2R 0RL, England
Penguin Group Ireland, 25 St. Stephen's Green, Dublin 2, Ireland (a division of Penguin Books Ltd.)
Penguin Group (Australia), 250 Camberwell Road, Camberwell, Victoria 3124, Australia
(a division of Pearson Australia Group Pty. Ltd.)
Penguin Books India Pvt. Ltd., 11 Community Centre, Panchsheel Park, New Delhi—110 017, India
Penguin Group (NZ), 67 Apollo Drive, Rosedale, North Shore 0632, New Zealand
(a division of Pearson New Zealand Ltd.)
Penguin Books (South Africa) (Pty.) Ltd., 24 Sturdee Avenue, Rosebank, Johannesburg 2196, South Africa

Penguin Books Ltd., Registered Offices: 80 Strand, London WC2R 0RL, England

FACES OF WAR

This book is an original publication of the Berkley Publishing Group.

A Lou Reda Book

Copyright © 2009 by Mark D. Faram and Lou Reda
Book design by Pauline Neuwirth

FIRST EDITION: May 2009

ISBN: 978-0-425-22140-2

PRINTED IN THE UNITED STATES OF AMERICA

10 9 8 7 6 5 4 3 2 1

ACKNOWLEDGMENTS

THIS BOOK WAS helped along by so many along the way that there's not enough room here to thank them all.

To Mr. Lou Reda, whose vision and guidance helped get this book noticed in the first place and to Natalee Rosenstein and Michelle Vega at Berkley Books whose patience with this first-time author was monumental.

In addition, I must thank Mr. Mike McLellan from the Navy Personnel Command in Millington, Tennessee, whose help in obtaining information from the service records of these men was invaluable and without that information, this book would not have been possible.

Likewise, to Mr. Chuck Haberline, who heads the Still Photo Section at the Navy Historical Center in Washington, D.C., for sharing his knowledge and allowing me the many long hours I spent going through the thousands of images in their collection.

To my great friends Bill Gunther and Meagan Fay, who opened up their home to me during my final push to complete the manuscript.

Finally, I'd like to thank those whose patience and gentle encouragement spurred me to actually complete this project including my parents, Harvey and Lois Faram, Ms. Valerie Robbins, and my loving daughters, Jonice and Sophia Faram.

CONTENTS

★   ★   ★

FOREWORD

PHOTOGRAPHY'S INVOLVEMENT IN our lives is infinite, an unblinking eye that holds forever tender moments of intimacy as well as the grand events of history. It is journalistic, scientific, artistic, historical, entertaining, and personal. Since its birth, photography has been a pervasive, compelling storyteller and keeper of the private and public record.

Edward Steichen's three-quarter-century love affair with the camera made broad use of photography's capacities. His remarkable talent and his acute sense of his time took him to more places than his contemporaries. *Faces of War* tells the story of that singular slice of Steichen's life and work in the U.S. Navy during World War II's Pacific campaign. Steichen, and his special collection of photographers, drew on decades of his experience, ranging from fine-art to high-fashion and even advertising photography, to produce enduring photos that even today tell us with clarity of that brutal conflict.

From the time Steichen was fifteen and taught himself how to use a camera, photography was his life. Born in Luxembourg in 1879 Steichen came to the United States as a young child, grew up in Michigan, and settled with his family in Milwaukee, where he worked as a lithographer, learning the technical details of visual reproduction. In his earliest days Steichen used his camera to support his ambitions as a painter and an illustrator.

Pictures made by the young photographer fell into the category photo historians called "Pictorialism"—scenes of various subjects from cityscapes to landscapes. Steichen, ever the experimenter, treated his lenses with petroleum jelly, used colored filters of various kinds, jiggled his tripod during exposures, and manipulated prints in the darkroom to produce unusual photographic effects and soft-focus prints.

At the same time he traveled back and forth between New York and Paris, dipping into the worlds of art and photography. World War I intervened and he returned permanently to New York, where he enlisted in the U.S. Army Signal Corps. He hoped to follow in the footsteps of Mathew Brady and photograph war's carnage and destruction. Instead he was assigned to organize a unit that specialized in aerial reconnaissance photography behind enemy lines, charting troop movements and installations. His Signal Corps work gave him an appreciation for strong, highly detailed photography that captured the vivid images needed for military intelligence work.

In a fit of reckless abandon he set fire to many of his paintings in 1922 and turned his attention to mastering the photographic process. One story tells how he photographed a cup and saucer with a black background more than a thousand times in order to completely understand the effect of lighting on a subject.

His postwar career blossomed, bringing him fame but also the sting of criticism from his fellow art photographers, who chastised him for going commercial. His pictures of fashion and celebrities were published in *Vogue* and *Vanity Fair*. He made portraits of the famous—Marlene Dietrich, Eugene O'Neill, J. P. Morgan, Greta Garbo, and Gloria Swanson, among others on a long list of headline makers. He produced advertising photography for the J. Walter Thompson Agency. In the 1920s and 1930s, Steichen became the highest paid and one of the best-known photographers in the United States.

Newer, younger photographers came on the scene, however, using smaller cameras to make pictures different from the startling photos that came from Steichen's studio. These pictures and their candid content captured attention and Steichen, though still America's premier photographer, closed his New York studio and retired from photography to pursue another of his lifelong ambitions—the cultivation and breeding of flowers.

Though he was acclaimed as one of the twentieth century's finest photographers, there were some who criticized his jumping from one format to another in the art, art photography, and commercial world. Broad but not deep, some said. His eclectic experience, as it turned out, however, would help him in his World War II assignment.

In the early days of the war, Steichen volunteered for duty in the U.S. military. He was sixty-two years old and his offer of service was challenged repeatedly, but he finally persuaded the Navy to take him aboard as director of the U.S. Naval Photographic Institute.

Steichen's experience enabled him to create a special unit of photographers who were up to the challenge set before him—to tell the story in pictures of the U.S. Navy's aerial activities. At this period, the U.S. Navy was a "battleship Navy." Aircraft carriers and the value of airpower were important but not a top priority. Still, the Navy needed to recruit some thirty thousand pilots to fly the fighters and bombers that would cripple the Japanese Navy on the far-flung islands and air bases of the Pacific Ocean. Steichen's task was to provide pictures that would help increase recruitment.

Steichen, who had moved successfully in the corporate world of New York media, knew that his photographers would need rank and the clout that goes with rank to gain access to picture possibilities, just as his contact with media moguls in New York helped his early efforts at big-time photography. Almost all photographers who joined his group would hold officer commissions, thus ensuring their access to transportation and information, access that was denied to enlisted photographers.

Steichen reached back into his experience and contacted skilled photographers with journalistic and advertising ability. They jumped at the opportunity to work with the old master in a new, challenging—and dangerous—photographic undertaking. He also recruited special technicians to keep his cameras working.

In about a year the crew was put together and photographed training sessions in the United States. Then came assignments to the Pacific, where the photographers joined carrier life at various and disparate locations. His instruction to them was to concentrate on the individuals and the details of their daily lives aboard the Navy's fighting ships.

Their pictures, carefully made, exquisitely composed, of the highest technical quality, sometimes personal and sometimes capturing the vast technical wonder of the carrier war, told the story of life on the battlefront of a vast ocean. The photos were popular in the United States, where Steichen again used his contacts in the media to push for their publication.

The Pacific war was different from the war in Europe, where tanks lumbered across muddy landscapes and GIs battled in mountains and towns. Refugees were everywhere, picking their way through the ruins of cities. The cities themselves were familiar to Americans—Rome, London, Paris, Berlin; the birthplaces of our culture and our ancestors. The Pacific offered great distances, where the only landmarks were the changing waves of an endless ocean. The locations—with names like Guadalcanal, Tarawa, Eniwetok, Peleliu—came with mysterious histories. Many were so small that they could not be found on most maps.

Pictures from the Steichen team captured the vast expanse of the Pacific, the seemingly endless waiting—waiting for planes to return from attacks on the enemy, waiting for enemy attacks on the carrier *Lexington,* scanning the horizon for incoming aircraft, be they friendly or hostile. Photographs showed bombing runs, exploding Japanese vessels, kamikaze attacks and the burning decks of aircraft carriers struck by bombs and planes, excited pilots returning from successful attacks on enemy carriers, and the solemn proceedings of burial at sea of those who died defending their ships.

Steichen himself spent months aboard the USS *Lexington* as she searched the Pacific for enemy targets. He was almost killed when a fighter spun out of control as he was photographing a landing. He was saved by leaping into a safety net that had been hung off the deck.

Steichen produced a book, *The Blue Ghost,* a chronicle of his days aboard the *Lexington,* along with the diary he kept while at sea. He edited a book entitled *U.S. Navy War Photographs* and another with his friend, editor Tom Maloney of

U.S. Camera, a popular photographic magazine of the period. The book contained large, well-printed photos from the Steichen group.

Wars end. The Steichen group was disbanded, leaving behind a legacy of some fifteen thousand compelling pictures of the world's greatest conflict.

In 1947, Steichen became the curator of photography at New York's Museum of Modern Art, a position he held until 1962. During this period, he and one of his Navy group, Wayne Miller, created photography's greatest exhibit, *The Family of Man,* which consisted of 503 photographs from sixty-eight nations that expressed the humanity that unites all the peoples of the world.

Author Mark Faram is uniquely qualified to bring together the Steichen story and the pictures his unit produced during World War II. The photos were scattered throughout the files of the national archives. Faram, a writer for the *Navy Times,* had access to the personnel jackets of the photographers Steichen gathered. He searched the picture files to find the best of their work for *Faces of War.*

HAL BUELL
Former head of the Associated Press international photo service
Groton, Connecticut
January 2009

Faces of War

INTRODUCTION

✶   ✶   ✶

IT WAS A military unit unlike any other in World War II. Still, when one hears the term *unit* or *outfit* in a military context, it often brings up mental images of men, side by side, fighting their way across Europe or hopping from island to island during the Pacific campaign.

But the Aviation Photographic Unit was not your father's outfit.

It was a band of visual storytellers, experts who worked alone, mostly thousands of miles apart, rarely interacting with one another.

Still, what made them a unit was that they were working toward a common goal. What brought their work together was the constant coaching, cajoling, and sometimes mentoring of legendary photographer Edward Steichen, who founded and led the unit.

Some experts have estimated that nearly fourteen thousand images created by the unit are currently in the collection of the National Archives. The work is historically significant not only as a visual record of the war but also for the impact it had in shaping the direction of photography and the careers of many photographers in the postwar years.

But because the images are not held together as a group by the government, at least not since the early 1960s, the work is largely untouched, and as a result, much of it has not been seen by the public since it was shot.

For this reason, what most Americans have seen of this work are just single, iconic images. Not the stories they were trying to tell or what they went through trying to tell them.

Also, with exclusive access to their military personnel records, much of who these photographers were and their wartime records has not been recounted in book form.

During World War II, the combined vision of the photographers in this unit gave Americans back home a glimpse into the lives of the people fighting the Navy's battles—whether it be a pilot, enlisted gunner, or sailor manning the deck of either an aircraft carrier or the rolling decks of destroyers, battleships, and submarines.

The unit started out with just six photographers and expanded to ten during the course of the war. Each photographer witnessed everything from the early aircraft raids to amphibious landings to the Japanese surrender in Tokyo Bay. Some of the men even went on special missions behind enemy lines, earning accolades and awards from the Navy brass for their work.

Steichen's entry into the Navy in 1942 at age sixty-two was nearly a miracle. In fact, he was initially rejected by the Navy's personnel office not only because of his age, but for health-related reasons—and it took high-powered intervention to even get him into uniform.

Had the aging photographer's application not been approved in the end, much of how America views the Navy's role in World War II would be significantly different.

Through Steichen's connections in the publishing world, the work of his photographers and many others in the service appeared in all the major newspapers and magazines around the country as well as in internal Navy publications.

After the war, the unit's work continued to be used to illustrate the war, though only as single images, without the context of their original stories.

Steichen's style was to guide the photographer's coverage in the field without micromanaging their individual work. The result was a picture of life in the Navy that was as diverse and dramatic as the personalities of the photographers themselves.

Though for most of the war he directed others from Washington, Steichen also led by example, heading to the front and shouldering cameras himself.

Once he was almost killed by an aircraft attempting to land on the aircraft carrier *Lexington* in the South Pacific.

Sending his photographers to war wasn't in his unit's original charter. Instead, they were to document naval aviation training around the country in order to coax young Americans into volunteering to fly aircraft wearing Navy blue instead of Army green. In addition, their images were needed for training books and movies.

But Steichen didn't stop there. He saw opportunity and his boundless energy made him jump in headfirst. As the war progressed, so did the scope of the unit's work. His unit went from being a part of the naval aviation "Training Aids" office to being recognized as the premier combat documentation unit in the Navy, with Steichen as the head of all naval photography.

That had been, in fact, his plan all along. This is the story of its realization.

A BRIEF HISTORY OF
NAVAL PHOTOGRAPHY

✶　　✶　　✶

EARLY NAVY PHOTOGRAPHERS weren't uniformed sailors. Instead, ship's captains would contract for commercial artists and photographers to accompany their ships and squadrons on voyages of any significance.

No one knows for sure when the first tripod and camera were lugged onboard a U.S. Navy vessel, but the first photographer of note to take on such an assignment was Eliphalet M. Brown, an accomplished daguerreotypist, lithographer, and artist who was in business in New York.

Daguerreotypes were produced through an early imaging process in which the plate exposed in the camera was also the finished product. No negative was produced, only a single, positive image.

Currier and Ives, then his employer, personally selected Brown in 1853 to accompany Commodore Matthew Perry during his historic visit to Japan, where he would negotiate the deal that

As the Navy's photographer on the Perry Expedition, Eliphalet M. Brown, Jr. is generally considered one of the first to photograph in Japan. Commodore Perry visited the newly opened port of Simoda from April 18 through May 9, 1854. This image of two women is a lithograph taken from one of Brown's images and is often identified as two geisha women.

eventually opened up that country for trade with the West.

Brown reportedly took more than four hundred images during the two-year expedition.

Although none of the images are known to have survived, nineteen of them were published in the government's official narrative of the expedition. They provide an excellent snapshot of the Japanese people and culture of the time. Brown, it seems, spent most of his time photographing the locals rather than the sailors.

Mathew Brady, the celebrated Civil War photographer, turned his cameras on the Navy in 1862 and exposed wet plates in photographing small groups of officers and men on the federal ironclad *Monitor* after its battle with the *Merrimac* at Hampton Roads, Virginia. They are the oldest "official Navy photographs" known today.

Officers and civilians at the Navy's Bureau of Ordnance did some minor photographic experiments in the late 1860s, but the cumbersome nature of their equipment made it difficult for shipboard use, and as a result, most images of the Navy before the turn of the century came from civilian commercial photographers.

Brown wasn't as skillful a photographer as he was an artist when he left on the expedition, but he quickly learned the trade. Slow film speeds required getting his subjects to sit still for long exposures, even in the light of day, and he seems to have communicated this to his subjects well.

Not surprisingly, picture taking in the Navy started in earnest after the turn of the century when Kodak began producing film that could be loaded in the daylight, and selling chemicals that made it easier to process those images outside of commercial labs.

Armed with these "Box Brownies," many enlisted sailors took on the job of "ship's photographer," usually with the official approval of their commanding officers.

But it wasn't a full-time job—these photographers did their picture taking in addition to their regular duty assignments and often sold their work to the ship's crew, pocketing the money themselves or sharing the profits with their captain.

Their job wasn't to officially document Navy life for the government, though some of their images did make their way to Navy headquarters in Washington, D.C., and can be seen today. These ship's photographers purchased their own gear and materials and ran private businesses onboard ship. This practice thrived until May 1918, when the Navy started issuing a Kodak camera and developing outfit to all ships and stations.

The town of Chew Lew was on modern-day Okinawa and was a stepping-off point for Perry on the way to China. In the narrative of the expedition, it explained the culture of the community and this image was used to illustrate the role of the men in a true documentary style that would have made Steichen smile. ". . . the men were the drones of the hive, and the women the workers." These three, the Chew Lew Gossips, were passing the time. "Once they had their fill of smoking and drinking tea they broke out the Saki and it was passed around . . . sometimes beyond the limits of prudence and discretion."

Many of these ship's photographers produced good work that survives today. One of them was Roy E. Wayne, officially Musician First Class, USN, who, in 1918, was sent with an official U.S. government mission to the Ukraine and southeastern Europe.

Officially, Wayne was a member of the admiral's band that moved with the official party and performed at events, but during the visit he also made approximately 2,400 photographs that were so good the Navy Department bought copies of many of them for official use.

Navy photography became an official job in 1921, but as early as 1916, sailors with talent had begun to work full-time in the profession on a regular basis.

The first photographic unit was organized in 1916 to document target

This lithograph is of the Temple at Tumai in Chew Lew done from a drawing by W. Heine, an expedition artist. In the center is expedition photographer, Eliphalet M. Brown, Jr., shown with his camera (dageurreotype).It is the only plate in the narrative that depicts Brown, who is photographing what would become the Chew Lew Gossips lithograph.

practice for ships. But the field unit would only take the pictures. The darkroom facilities were located in a building at the Washington, D.C., Navy Yard.

World War I proved to the world that aerial photography was crucial to wartime intelligence efforts, and the scramble was on in both the Army and Navy to develop expertise in that skill in the ranks.

In December 1917, the Bureau of Navigation, Navy Department, sent a telegram to all ships and stations. It read: "Require for expert photographic work connection aviation, men of high mental attainments and have knowledge photography period men selected will be given special instruction under expert supervision."

The service began to commission as officers some of the men who had been working as ship's photographers.

These new photo officers established the Navy's first photo school at U.S. Naval Air Station, Miami, Florida, where the first six-week course started in March 1918 with six enlisted students. By the end of the war, four classes had graduated, giving the Navy's photo community a total of nine officers and eighty enlisted men.

The sailors were given the rating of aviation printer (photographer) and wore on their rating badge with their rank the open-book insignia of naval printer, the service's lithographers.

Unofficially, some of the men had naval aviation wings embroidered onto their badges on either side of the open book and were quickly called "flying preachers" because their job was aerial reconnaissance, and as enlisted men rather than pilots, they didn't rate gold Navy pilots' wings.

Photography officially came into its own in July of 1921, when the Navy finally decided to make photography a formal rating. Not only was the rating of photographer created, but an embroidered camera for sailors to wear with their rank on their sleeve was approved as well—but not with wings.

Before World War II, photography was an enlisted man's job. Naval officers, even the ones commissioned from the ranks of the photographers, just didn't carry the heavy cameras and tripods the profession required. It was simply not a gentleman's job.

This was the attitude that Steichen encountered when he entered the Navy and had the audacity to suggest that there be commissioned photographers who carried their own cameras. It goes without saying that this suggestion did not sit well with the rank-and-file Navy photographers.

Lieutenant Commander Edward Steichen, in full General Quarters battle gear, observes operations from the bridge of the aircraft carrier Lexington *during operations against the Japanese-held Marcus Islands in November 1943.*

CHAPTER 1

The Old Man

★　　★　　★

THERE ARE FEW PLACES on earth more dangerous than a flight deck, but that's where Edward Steichen wanted to be. That's where the action always was . . .

It was November 9, 1943, on board the aircraft carrier *Lexington*. The ship was steaming toward battle in the South Pacific with the Japanese fleet.

Steichen, armed only with a camera, his favorite Kodak Medalist, was watching aircraft line up to make their landings on deck—documenting what it takes to get aircraft back on the ship.

He was kneeling next to Lieutenant Dave Butler, one of the *Lexington*'s landing signal officers, or "paddles," as the circling pilots call them—a reference to the two multicolored paddles they hold in their hands to direct the pilots down from the sky and help them land their planes safely on deck.

The two officers were as far back aft on the ship as possible and exposed to the elements, as well as to the landing planes. Below them was only a mesh safety net, and below that the blue waters of the Pacific Ocean.

Steichen was lining up his shot—a blurred aircraft landing—behind Butler as Butler waved his paddles.

"I shifted position for a less vertical angle, and hear the call that the incoming plane is ok," Steichen said. "I've lined up my shot and I'm waiting."

But things weren't okay, and the aircraft was sliding to the left—directly toward Steichen and Butler.

In a flash, the blue sky in Steichen's camera's viewfinder suddenly turned into a blue-gray onrushing mass as the aircraft came swooping nearly on top of them.

Lieutenant Commander Edward Steichen in his favorite perch under an overhang on the island of the aircraft carrier Lexington. *Steichen would spend hours on his perch observing during operations against the Japanese-held Marcus Islands in November 1943.*

"Instinctively, I press the shutter button, and immediately I am knocked flat in the net and the two landing signal officers land on top of me," Steichen said.

Looking up, Steichen could see the tail of the aircraft hanging above him. It had broken off the aircraft as the plane crashed into the ship's flight deck, and was dangling just a few feet above him and the other officers, gasoline pouring from ruptured fuel lines like a waterfall.

"Let's get the hell out of here," Butler yelled to Steichen, and in a moment the two men were back up on deck, running toward the ship's "island" super-structure as the remains of the Hellcat fighter tumbled from the ship and into the water, her pilot still strapped in his seat.

Rushing down the deck to meet Steichen, who at age sixty-three was the oldest man on the ship, was the executive officer, Commander B. W. Wright, who had watched the crash unfold from the bridge, halfway up the island.

"How are you, old-timer?" Wright asked Steichen while reaching out to grasp the photographer's hand with both of his.

"That was a pretty close shave," Steichen said, shaking the commander's hand.

"Man, you just can't have a closer one," Wright continued, still holding on to Steichen's hand.

"Yeah, but I got the shot anyway," Steichen finished.

That's what it was all about—getting the shot. That's what Steichen believed he had been brought into the Navy to do, and he was feeling like a young man again, flirting with death to document a war.

But being on the front lines, or heading toward them, wasn't what Captain Arthur Radford thought the famous photographer would be doing for him when he'd fought to get Steichen onto active duty just two years earlier.

America had just formally entered World War II, though the nation had been gearing up for the fight for the past couple of years. Now that America had been attacked, mobilization efforts were in high gear.

Radford was head of the training literature division of the U.S. Navy's Bureau of Aeronautics in Washington, D.C., a position he had assumed just days after the Japanese bombed Pearl Harbor on December 7, 1941.

An experienced aviator, Radford was in charge of stocking the Navy's aircraft carriers and squadrons with qualified pilots who could fly and the enlisted men who were needed to maintain those aircraft and the ordnance they carried.

It was clear to Radford that this would be a different kind of naval war from any in history. Gone was the heyday of the battleship, though this war would still prove them valuable. Mostly they would turn their massive guns on enemy troops and positions ashore instead of enemy ships on the high seas.

It was a lesson the Japanese had proven to the world on December 7, with their over-the-horizon dawn attack on the U.S. Pacific Fleet at Pearl Harbor—and one Americans would have to learn and emulate if they wanted to turn the tide of battle in the Pacific.

This meant that the Navy would have to build fast carriers and man them with top-notch aviators. To get such men they would have to compete with the Army's Air Corps. Radford's early estimates called for at least thirty thousand new pilots a year. It was gearing up to be a war for people—one Radford wanted to win. He wanted Steichen in uniform, finding ways to tell the story of naval aviation in the mainstream media in order to spur recruiting efforts.

The problem was that Steichen was sixty-two years old, beyond the normal age for induction into military service. Getting him into Navy blue was shaping up to be a battle in itself.

By 1941, the aging Steichen had become a mainstay on the American photographic scene, where many in the field had dubbed him the "Dean of American Photography."

Born on March 27, 1879 in Luxembourg, as Edouard Jean Steichen, he moved with his family at an early age to Hancock, Michigan, where his father worked in a copper mine.

At age fifteen, he moved on to Milwaukee, Wisconsin, to attend Pio Nono College, a Catholic high school and college founded as a school for teachers. It was here that his talent for art was discovered.

Initially, it was his drawings that showed artistic promise. He quit school in 1894 to work full-time as an apprentice designer for the American Fine Art Company in Milwaukee. The firm specialized in corporate work, designing and printing posters and advertising cards for local brewers, flour mills, and pork packers.

His interest in photography took a major leap when, in 1895, his mother gave him enough money to purchase his first camera. His initial plan was to use photography as an aid for his advertising design work.

A local camera-store owner sold him the first camera Steichen ever held and told the young man it was a "detective camera." Actually, it was one of the original Kodak box cameras that became popular in the 1890s by offering consumers the promise that "you press the button, we do the rest."

"I believed the roll contained 50 exposures," Steichen recalled in his autobiography, *A Life in Photography*. "This was an appalling thing in itself, because it meant that I would not see what I was doing until I had made fifty pictures."

That first roll of film produced only one photograph that could be printed; the rest, he was told by the owner of the photo shop, were not exposed correctly and thus unusable.

"I don't remember ever having made another roll with the detective camera," Steichen wrote. He quickly returned the camera and purchased a 4X5 camera that allowed him to shoot one film plate at a time and learn the craft more quickly and without shelling out too much money.

Gradually, by trial and error, he began to get the hang of photography. But he didn't see it as an art form in and of itself. It was mainly a way to produce images for his drawing and painting.

By 1900, the promising young artist had given up work at the lithographic company and headed to Europe to study painting—though he always had a parallel interest in photography and progressed in both disciplines.

Stopping first in New York, he met Alfred Steiglitz, then arguably the most famous photographer in America and an advocate of the view that photography was an art form in its own right, a view Steichen now shared. The two became fast friends.

The relationship would last for years, but became tempestuous as Steichen's fame came to rival that of his early mentor and friend. When Steichen moved away from artistic photography into the world of advertising and magazine work, Steiglitz believed he had sold out. Steichen looked at it as a natural progression in his work.

Over the next decade and a half, he would split his time between Paris and New York, polishing his skills as a painter and photographer.

Most thought of Steichen as a painter first. But gradually, photography became his primary art and his early style in the medium gradually developed.

He made dark portraits of the sculptor Auguste Rodin, President Theodore Roosevelt, and industrialist J. P. Morgan, to name just a few—all jobs he took to support himself and his growing family, which now included his first wife, Clara, whom he married in 1903, and their two daughters, Mary and Kate, born in 1904 and 1908.

The portrait that made Steichen famous. In 1903, then-twenty-seven-year-old Edward Steichen had two minutes to photograph famous businessman J. P. Morgan. Morgan liked the photograph so much, he paid Steichen $500 apiece for ten copies—the most money paid for a photograph at that time.

He dabbled in what would later become a mainstay of his work—fashion photography—and took an early stab at what he would become famous for in World War II—documentary photography.

"One day in the summer of 1907, I borrowed from a friend a German hand camera," Steichen later recalled of the first time he went out with a portable camera to capture unposed shots at the French racetrack in Longchamps. "Armed with this camera I made my first serious attempt at documentary reportage."

Instead of photographing the horses, though, his eye focused on the high-fashion and social details of the event. The images he produced are considered an excellent portrait of French social life in the early 1900s, though he didn't continue doing much handheld documentary work after that.

As the twentieth century moved into its second decade, Steichen achieved critical acclaim as both a painter and a photographer.

His early work was impressionistic in its technique, often using special chemicals and techniques that made his images look like drawings and paintings. As time passed, his photographs became more "straight" in nature, that is, sharper in focus and higher in contrast. His subject matter came to be portrayed in a very straightforward way.

Steichen lived outside Paris in the town of Voulangis, where he not only painted but spent a great deal of time cultivating a garden of delphiniums, a pastime he would enjoy for the rest of his life.

It was here that his life changed almost overnight as Europe plunged headlong into World War I.

"Everyone's life changed in twenty-four hours," Steichen wrote of his first experience with war. "Horses were requisitioned and every foreigner was suspected as a spy." As the Germans closed in on Paris, he and his family fled to New York, leaving just two days before advanced patrols of the German army reached his home.

As entry into the war grew closer for the United States, so did Steichen's interest in photographing that war.

"I wanted to get into the war on the American side," he said. "I wanted to be a photographic reporter, as Mathew Brady had been in the Civil War." So, for the first time, Steichen made the trip from New York to Washington, D.C., to offer his services to the Army.

It was also his first experience with outright rejection. At thirty-eight, he was six years older than the Army normally allowed for initial induction into service. But Army officials saw photography as a great potential source of intelligence and the service had no experts in the ranks. Steichen's age was waived

14TH PHOTO SECTION – 1ST ARMY
THE BALLOONATIC SECTION

E–4292
C–1052 400142

During World War I, Steichen joined the American Expeditionary Forces as a photographic expert. When given a choice, he chose to serve in the Photographic Section of the Air Service, where he would become the commanding officer and rise to the rank of Lieutenant Colonel. Under him were fifty-five officers, a thousand men. They flew over German lines and "shot" the enemy territory. Here he poses, fifth from the left in the front row, with the balloon section of his service in 1918.

and he entered the Army as a first lieutenant in the Signal Corps on July 16, 1917. That day, he forever changed his name from the European Edouard Jean to the American Edward John.

But his ideas of documenting war on the ground for posterity would wait another quarter of a century before being realized. During his initial training after induction, he became interested in aerial photography and quickly grasped its rising value to military leaders as a source of intelligence on enemy troop positions and strength.

His decision to pursue aerial intelligence led to his being among the first American troops to land in France with General John J. "Black Jack" Pershing.

Steichen often flew on photo missions and took many images himself such as this aerial view of ruins of Vaux, France, taken in March 1918. It was the stark realism of images like this that led him to shift from more impressionistic photo work before the war to a much more realistic style that led to his success in advertising and magazine work.

"Aerial photographs are by far the most important, as they have become in modern warfare the chief source of information as to the position, disposition and movements of the enemy all the way from the front line trenches to the most remote rear area," he wrote in a report filed at the end of the war. "No maps, however accurate they may be, will give as correct an idea of the terrain and objectives as can be gained from good technical aerial photographs."

He was promoted to captain while in France and then to major two days after the war ended, and stayed on in France until his discharge from active duty on October 13, 1919. In December of the same year, he was promoted to lieutenant colonel in the reserves and often used that title, even including it with his listing in the New York City phone book.

His movement into more realistic photography continued after the war. He pioneered photography in advertising and photographed the nation's and world's famous for *Vogue* and *Vanity Fair,* work that succeeded in making him almost as famous as his subjects.

For the next nineteen years, he worked out of his New York studio, sometimes employing as many as seven assistants. In 1938, he retired suddenly to experiment in color photography and grow delphiniums at his new Connecticut home.

With Europe again at war, Steichen's mind returned to the idea of documenting the conflict. He intended to reactivate his old commission as a lieutenant colonel, which had officially terminated in December of 1924 due to lack of service. Hopeful he could again be in uniform, he traveled to Washington in the fall of 1941.

"Sorry, Mr. Steichen, but you are just too old for induction into active service," said an Army clerk as he wrote down the aging photographer's birth date after he

Steichen's portrait work for Vanity Fair *set the standard for Hollywood and celebrity portraiture in the 1920s and 1930s. Here, he shot Greta Garbo in 1928 in his New York studio. It was work like this that cemented Steichen's reputation in the photographic world and gave him the credibility to gain a commission in the Navy at age sixty-two.*

showed up unannounced at Army headquarters. Steichen was crushed. A few months later, on December 7, 1941, that defeat would feel like an open wound when the United States was attacked by the empire of Japan.

"Then, more than ever," he wrote in his autobiography, "I felt my disappointment at not being readmitted."

Undaunted, he clung to his dream of documenting a war on the ground and somehow photograph the conflict and the country's efforts to mobilize.

It wasn't just portraiture that made Steichen famous; his advertising work, included architecture work such as this 1932 photo he called "The Maypole," which was, in fact, the Empire State Building in New York City.

"I thought my only chance to be of service in photography was as a civilian," Steichen said. He had begun to pursue that idea in the fall of 1941.

Since his service in World War I, he'd held to the idealistic belief that if the general public could see the horrors firsthand through photography, the resulting outcry might help eliminate war forever, or at least make leaders think twice before starting them.

So he began to try to organize groups of civilian photographers to blanket the country and produce a photographic record of the nation's war mobilization.

His luck began to change. First, David McAlpin, a trustee of the Museum of Modern Art, approached Steichen with the idea of putting together a photo exhibit at the New York museum that would highlight America's national defense buildup. The show would be called *The Arsenal of Democracy*.

Faced with sitting out the war, Steichen saw the exhibition as a chance to help create national unity. After Pearl Harbor, the project was renamed *The Road to Victory*.

Selection of the images and organization of the exhibit occupied much of his next six months, during which Steichen's effort to get back into uniform would take a new turn.

Even as Captain Radford sought ways to get publicity for naval aviation, Steichen's personal network expanded into the Navy's ranks as trustee McAlpin joined the Navy and was assigned to its Bureau of Aeronautics.

Captain Arthur Radford photographed by Lieutenant Commander Edward Steichen at the Bureau of Aeronautics in Washington, D.C., in 1942. Radford was instrumental in getting Steichen commissioned and getting his Aviation Photographic Unit off the ground. Steichen took portraits of many of the Navy's brass in an effort to make contacts for his photographers to get access to Navy Units.

In addition, Eugene Meyer, then the publisher of the *Washington Post* and a longtime friend, brought Steichen's talents and desires to the attention of then Undersecretary of the Navy James Forrestal.

No official record exists of exactly how Steichen finally got his foot in the Navy's door in early January 1942, but that it happened is a matter of record—and just when Steichen believed all hope was lost.

"I received a telephone call from the Navy Department in Washington asking me if I would be interested in photographing for the Navy," he said. "I almost crawled through the telephone wire with eagerness."

Not one to waste time, Steichen was on a train to Washington that evening and turned up at the Bureau of Aeronautics at the crack of dawn. The white-haired photographer was quickly ushered into Radford's office.

"When I walked into Radford's office, I saw a look of surprise on his face," Steichen said. "He had apparently not been informed that I was no longer a young man."

Fearing a repeat of the Army's rejection, he knew he had to think fast. Just then Radford's phone rang, giving Steichen time to gather his thoughts while the naval officer took care of business.

"The moment Captain Radford hung up, I started talking fast," Steichen said.

Stressing his World War I experience with the Army Air Corps and his relationship with aviation legend General Billy Mitchell and with General Pershing, he quickly outlined his plan.

"I told him I would like to head up a small unit of half a dozen photographers, commissioned by the Navy, to photograph the story of naval aviation during the war," he said.

The more Radford expanded on the idea, the more interested Steichen became, forgetting all about the old photographer's age for the moment.

Here was the solution to Radford's problem. With his media contacts, Steichen could oversee the production and release of images and stories that could quickly tell the story of naval aviation to the country. In addition, his work could be used in the training materials the service would need to teach their growing force.

Steichen's next stop was the office of the assistant secretary of the Navy for air, Artemus Gates, a naval aviator and hero during World War I and a successful banker after the war who was connected at all levels of business and government.

Gates, too, was surprised by Steichen's age, but after hearing the famous photographer's ideas, he was also impressed and gave Radford the go-ahead to try to bring Steichen on active duty.

Now the battle would begin to get the Navy's personnel bureaucrats to agree.

His application for a commission in the Naval Reserve was dated January 19,1942, and was quickly endorsed and sent on to Washington.

Radford and Gates had left together on January 20 for an inspection tour of the training facilities at Naval Air Station, Corpus Christi, Texas. Both men were confident that Steichen's commission would be approved quickly. Radford had a back channel memo sent to the Navy's Bureau of Navigation, which was responsible for all the service's personnel functions, asking them to "waive some of the customary routine" and speed approval of the commission.

Edward Steichen's side-view portrait taken from his application for a commission into the U.S. Navy in January 1942.

Edward Steichen's front-view portrait taken from his application for a commission into the U.S. Navy in January 1942.

That's when the application ground to a sudden halt, on January 22, when the results of Steichen's physical examination had been processed and were being considered by a special board of examiners at the Navy Department.

"Edward John Steichen is found NOT physically qualified for appointment in [the] U.S. Naval Reserve by reason of defective vision [though correctable to 20/20], insufficient teeth, moderate sclerosis [hardening of the arteries] and tachycardia [too rapid a pulse]," wrote Rear Admiral Ross T. McIntire, the Navy's surgeon general, in a memorandum endorsing the board's rejection of Steichen's application to Vice Admiral Randall Jacobs, head of the Bureau of Navigation and the Navy's top personnel admiral.

The next day, requests for waivers for Steichen came from all levels of the Navy. Gates sent a personal note to Jacobs stating that "the desirability of obtaining Mr. Steichen's services warrant[s] granting a waiver of his physical defects. If at all possible, I shall appreciate this being done."

But still the Navy's personnel bureaucracy threw up roadblocks as one of Jacobs's deputies wrote back that Steichen was not only not physically qualified, he was twelve years over the age of fifty, the oldest age the service allowed anyone to join.

"To appoint this applicant would set a precedent which would be very embarrassing for the Bureau of Navigation," wrote Captain V. D. Chapline in a January 28 memorandum. "Many eminent men have voluntarily offered their services during the present emergency and have been denied commissions in the Naval Reserve due to age or physical conditions."

Chapline's solution was that Steichen should be "utilized in a civilian capacity," an idea that was unacceptable to Gates and Radford.

Finally Gates took the problem up his chain of command, through Forrestal to Secretary of the Navy Frank Knox, who gave Jacobs a personal call in order to resolve the solution.

Reluctantly, on January 28, Jacobs gave ground and agreed to bring Steichen on active duty. He scribbled a note in his own hand to "waive and comply, by direction SecNav" on the bureau's own rejection memo of Steichen.

That same day, Chapline, now acting reluctantly on Jacobs's orders, sent Steichen notice of a "waiver of your physical defects," as well as one for age.

The plan, according to an office memorandum, was first to bring Steichen in as a lieutenant commander, with the idea that "promotion to the rank of commander [would] follow as soon as it is practicable."

Undersecretary Gates also penned a personal note to Steichen around the same time saying "we are all delighted that you are going to join the Navy, and I look forward to seeing you on active duty soon."

Finally on January 30, the paperwork was all done and the Navy issued Steichen's commission in the Naval Reserve. The photographer, who had been informed by phone, was already hard at work framing out his unit.

Lieutenant Commander Edward Steichen, photographed in February, just days after accepting his commission into the U.S. Navy. The image was done while Steichen was working on The Road To Victory *exhibit in New York.*

Shortly after landing back on the aircraft carrier Yorktown, *Lieutenant Charles Kerlee, carrying two K-20 aerial cameras, steps down from a Grumman TBF-1 Avenger. Kerlee had stood behind the pilot of the aircraft for four hours during a raid on Wake Island on October 6, 1943.*

CHAPTER 2

The First Arrivals: Steichen Builds His Team

★　　　★　　　★

WAYNE MILLER WAS already in the Navy and working at the Bureau of Aeronautics in Washington, D.C., when Steichen's commission finally went through.

Miller was just out of college when he joined the Navy in late 1941. He had reported to its Bureau of Aeronautics as a brand-new ensign in early 1942 shortly after completing officer indoctrination school.

Unlike Steichen, Miller wasn't brought in to take pictures. As a young ensign, he was required to go where "the needs of the Navy were." At the time he reported to Washington, that need was for an officer in charge of the classified material vault, deep in the bowels of the bureau.

"It was like a very large safe and there was correspondence and other materials just stacked all over the place," he said. "It was a mess and my job was to organize the mess so people could find what they needed."

Sorting papers, even classified ones, wasn't Miller's idea of a good time. But he put his best into the project and within a month had the place organized and running smoothly.

What he really wanted was to be a photographer. In college, he'd picked up a camera and was instantly hooked. Upon arriving in Washington, he showed his small portfolio of images to anyone who expressed the slightest interest.

One of these people was a woman named Joy Bright Hancock, head of public affairs for the bureau at the beginning of the war.

Lieutenant Wayne Miller, a budding photographer who was already working at the Bureau of Aeronautics when Steichen got his commission, put the unit together, and it grew the most during the war under Steichen's direction. The two would remain friends until the elder's death in the early 1970s. Here, he relaxes late in the war on board the carrier Ticonderoga in the South Pacific.

She'd been a chief yeoman in the Navy during World War I and a civilian employee working for the Navy since 1930. Twice she'd married Navy pilots and twice she'd been widowed by aircraft crashes.

Still, she became a private pilot in order to overcome her fears of flying and as a result became a key player in the Bureau of Aeronautics during the years leading up to the war. Later in 1942, she became a driving force to get women into uniform in World War II. Eventually she rose to the rank of captain.

Dressed out in shipboard battle gear, including antiflash mask and canvas gauntlet gloves, Lieutenant Wayne Miller prepares to photograph combat operations off the Philippines in late 1944.

Hancock knew about Steichen and his pending arrival. When she saw Miller's work, she thought the young ensign would be a good fit for Steichen's project.

"Hancock encouraged me to show my images to Radford," Miller said. "In fact she took them up there herself to show him and I was summoned [to his office] a few minutes later."

After going over the images, Radford turned to Miller with a thoughtful look in his eye. "We have a photographer coming in soon to do some pictures," he told Miller. "His name is Steichen or Stuchen or Stoooken—something like that—anyway, maybe there's a place for you in this organization he's setting up."

Radford told Miller that Steichen was in New York preparing a photo show on national defense at the Museum of Modern Art, one that would show the Navy's and the nation's resolve in the war, but that he was ultimately coming to the bureau to form a special unit.

"I heard this name, and it just sent chills down my back," Miller said. "Everybody who had much interest in photography at that time knew who Steichen was and to think this guy was coming in the Navy and maybe I could meet him and even work with him was an incredible thought."

Miller had never even been to New York, and now he wanted to go in the worst way.

"I lied and told Radford that I had planned to go up to New York over the weekend anyway and he gave me permission to go up immediately and show my photographs to Steichen," he said. "I called and made an appointment to meet Steichen and then got on the train and headed north. I was just a nervous kid, full of hope and optimism. What I didn't know [was] that this was going to change my life forever."

Miller met the old man at the offices of *U.S. Camera* magazine, where Steichen and Tom Maloney, the magazine's editor, were poring over images for the next issue.

Though Steichen wasn't officially on staff, he'd developed a relationship with the magazine over the years, often as a contributor of images, but was increasingly becoming a guest editor as well.

When Steichen "retired" from his studio in 1938, his role in the magazine expanded. The relationship would continue throughout the war, with *U.S Camera* becoming a regular publisher of the Steichen unit's works.

On the day of Miller's visit, Steichen stepped away from the editing table, sat down with the young ensign, and looked over his images, carefully considering each one.

"We'll make arrangements to get you transferred over to my unit we're putting together," Steichen told him.

"I was so proud I had been accepted by the great Steichen to be a photographer in his special unit," Miller said. "I felt like I had arrived in the world."

Thirty years later, shortly before Steichen's death, Miller asked the old man about that day and just what was it about his images that had caught his eye.

"Nothing at all, they were terrible, really terrible," Steichen said. "What caught my eye was that you were young, enthusiastic, and I needed somebody like that to help me out getting the unit off the ground—the fact you later turned to an excellent photographer after that was a bonus."

Miller returned to Washington and went to work getting the material and supplies together for the unit.

And that's when the battles with the Navy's existing photographic community started as well. The irony is the Navy's photographic leadership was also under the auspices of the Bureau of Aeronautics; thus it was easy for Radford to squash the opposition to Steichen and his unit.

"The under-the-table idea was to publicize naval aviation in competition for pilots and gunners and crewmen," Miller said. "So under the guise of creating training materials, for use within the service, we were to produce images which would make the Navy look as exciting as possible to new recruits."

Steichen quickly realized the benefits of working outside the Navy's regular photographic and public-relations community, which is why he was excited when Radford and Gates decided his unit would operate out of the Bureau's Training Literature Division, over which Radford had direct control.

"We also discovered that it was easier to get funding for what we needed under the name of 'training,'" Miller said. "Especially early in the war, fewer questions were asked."

All this is why the Steichen unit started the war officially as the "Training Literature Field Unit No. 1," though that title was used only in official correspondence such as orders and requisitions. The unit quickly became known popularly as the Naval Aviation Photographic Unit, a title that has unofficially stuck down through the years.

Not much is known about Lieutenant Dwight Long, recruited from Hollywood by Steichen to do motion picture projects for the unit.

The first few months of the war, Steichen worked out of New York, gathering images for *The Road to Victory* exhibit. But at the same time he was recruiting experienced photographers for his unit that was now forming down in Washington, D.C.

Steichen had convinced Radford that most of his photographers needed to be officers. While he easily persuaded Radford and Gates, the Navy's regular photographic community thought this was blasphemy. Photographic officers were administrators and not shooters. It was not "officer-like" to carry cameras, in their view.

But Steichen's argument prevailed, and the allure of an officer's commission as well as the promise of unlimited access to the Navy allowed Steichen to recruit from among the nation's best and brightest photographers.

Also, Steichen deliberately sought out photographers from a wide range of disciplines, including advertising, illustration, and magazine, as well as experts in documentary and newspaper photography, to join the unit.

"In planning this work originally, I attached considerable importance to differences in personality and to the variety of their talents in the belief that the final document would, as a result, present not any one point of view, but a balanced pictorial symposium leading to an objectivity no one photographer could obtain," Steichen wrote after the war.

The wide range in experience and skills baffled even the members of the unit.

"Off duty, almost every one of them sooner or later came to me separately and said he understood why he had been chosen for the job, but he couldn't understand why some of the others had been," Steichen wrote in his autobiography.

His goal was to create a unit that could not only carry out the original mission of the unit, that of supplying the Navy with images for aviation training literature, but could also realize Steichen's dream of documenting the Navy at war.

By the end of the summer of 1942, he'd completed the recruiting of the original members of his unit. Two of his most sought-after recruits never made it into Navy blue, however.

In the spring of that year, Steichen had personally escorted Arthur Rothstein on a tour of the Washington facilities he was developing. At the time, Rothstein was working for *Look* magazine. He had made his reputation in the 1930s documenting the Depression for the Farm Security Administration. To this day, he and the photographers he worked with on this project are considered to have set the standard for documentary photo work.

After the tour, Rothstein was convinced of the importance of Steichen's unit and applied to the Navy for a commission.

But to his and Steichen's chagrin, he was rejected for being too short. Naval aviation, it seemed, had strict rules on height and not even Steichen with his connections could get him a waiver. Rothstein joined the Army's Signal Corps instead.

Another future photographic legend got a similar rejection from the Navy's medical examiners.

W. Eugene Smith, who would later become a legend at *Life* magazine, was excited about the prospect of working for Steichen. But he had recently been injured by explosions while covering Army maneuvers, and though he was expected to recover, no appeal from Steichen would cause the Navy to change its mind.

Charles Kerlee started out working in a motion picture film developing laboratory and grew into one of the most successful commercial and advertising photographers on the West Coast. He also taught photography in Los Angeles and produced his own instructional book.

"Although Eugene Smith appears to be a genius in his field, he does not measure up to Naval standards," the Navy's medical examination board wrote to Steichen.

Undaunted, Smith would go to war as a civilian with Steichen's help, and eventually produced some of *Life* magazines most iconic images.

It was from the ranks of *Life*'s young photographers that Steichen found two of the first three photographers for his unit.

First into uniform was Charles E. Kerlee, who at the time was one of the most well-known advertising photographers on the West Coast, working out of his Hollywood studio.

Kerlee's selection seemed like a natural one for Steichen, who himself had been among the elite advertising photographers in the nation in the 1930s. But despite that fact, it was Steichen's friend Tom Maloney at *U.S. Camera* who had to convince him that Kerlee was a good selection, as the two men had never met.

Though he accepted Steichen's invitation in February 1942, it wasn't until March 26 that Kerlee's commission finally came through and yet another month of indoctrination before he reported to Steichen in Washington.

At age thirty-four, he'd been working in photography since he graduated from the University of Southern California's School of Cinematography in 1929 and went to work at the MGM studios.

He started out on the ground floor, working in the film developing department, eventually working his way up to the camera department, of which, by 1931, he had become the assistant head.

He moved on to work at the R-K-O studios in 1932, where he continued his motion camera work in the special effects department. It was here that he developed his interest in still photography.

"During this time, I worked at nights at my home and attended art school, studying and developing my photographic technique," Kerlee wrote in 1941 as part of his application to join the Navy. "I finally decided to specialize in [still] illustrative photography and in 1935 left R-K-O to start my own business."

That business quickly took off and soon he was very busy with clients from all over the country.

"We believe him to be the best photographer on the Pacific Coast and one of the best in the United States," wrote William O. Chessman, the art editor at *Collier's* magazine in New York in a letter of recommendation to the Navy. "Our only regret is that his services will be lost to *Collier's* during his period of service with the Navy."

Other clients produced similar sentiments.

"Mr. Kerlee is ideally suited to serve his country in any capacity connected with photography," wrote W. Johns of the MacManus, John and Adams advertising agency in Detroit, for whom Kerlee had worked on numerous automobile advertising accounts. "He will get along with people and he handles subordinates well," Johns added in a postscript.

What his clients praised most was Kerlee's technical expertise, as well as his ability to pass that knowledge on to others. Not only was he a regular lecturer at the Art Center School in Los Angeles, he had also published a textbook in 1938 about photo illustration. Entitled *Pictures with a Purpose—How They Are Made*, it was highly praised in photographic circles.

But getting into uniform wasn't smooth sailing for Kerlee, either. Though he had been an early pioneer in the use of color photography in both motion picture and still work, he failed the color-blindness test during his Navy physical. But unlike his experience with Smith and Rothstein, Steichen was able to get Kerlee a waiver.

Kerlee was commissioned as a lieutenant, the third rank up the officer ladder, because of his experience, saving him from the inglorious life of an ensign in the Navy—a position many consider the worst in the service.

He arrived in Washington on May 28, 1942, and reported for work at the Bureau of Aeronautics on June 1.

A former merchant seaman and air-conditioning mechanic, Jacobs came to photography from the real estate business. His ability to tackle industrial subjects and still bring a human element to them was crucial to the Steichen unit. Jacobs is shown here in the application photos included in his commission package to the Navy.

Kerlee's induction into the unit was followed closely by that of the colorful Charles Fenno Jacobs.

Anyone who got to know Jacobs found him to have a dry sense of humor. He considered himself a gourmet chef and liked to drink very old brandy.

Excluding Steichen himself, Jacobs was the oldest photographer recruited into the unit. He was thirty-seven when he was commissioned a lieutenant in the Naval Reserve on April 11, 1942.

His formal education ended with his high school graduation, so when war broke out, he lacked the college diploma normally required to get an officer's commission in the U.S. Navy—and readily admitted this fact on his application.

"It's the first time I've been confronted with the slender record of my academic career," Jacobs wrote in a three-page essay in which he argued that the Navy should allow him in as an officer and a photographer. "However, the whole matter was one of my own choosing and one which, up to this moment, I have never regretted."

But he'd gotten quite an education in life by the time World War II broke out, and was on his fifth career when he joined the Navy.

His working life began at age nineteen, when he followed his father into the heating business as a card-carrying union steamfitter's helper.

Two years later, in 1925, he took a job as a sales engineer in Boston, where for the next three years, he prospered, until his company merged with several others in the same line of work and his job was eliminated.

"I was very successful in that job and would probably still be working there had it not been for that merger," he wrote.

World War II and the Navy was not Fenno's first experience at going to sea.

In 1929, he spent a little over a year working merchant ships as a seaman, making runs to the Mediterranean, first as an ordinary seaman and later as an able-bodied seaman.

As a result, his Navy record states he had "extensive experience" with "navigation in coastal waters and [was] adept at handling small boats in these kinds of waters."

By 1931, he was back at work as a heating sales engineer, this time in New York. But with the Depression in full swing, that wouldn't last long.

"Building construction was at a standstill and there was no market for the things I sold and prospects were dismal," he wrote. "Anything seemed a better bet and I went into the real estate business . . . specializing in Wall Street office space."

For the next three years, Jacobs managed to make what he called a "nominal living." But that success came at a high cost. "Considering the times, [making a living] was something of an accomplishment," he wrote. "However, I detested the work and was completely miserable during it all."

It was his discovery of photography that made life livable again. In 1932, at

Lieutenant Commander Charles Fenno Jacobs poses on board the battleship New Jersey *during operations in the South Pacific in December 1944.*

age twenty-eight, he purchased a Leica and began spending hours wandering New York City, "taking photos as my fancy willed of the things I saw," he wrote.

Despite his dislike for the real estate business, he never let it show in his photographic work. It did, however, quickly become evident to his employer that Jacobs's interest and talents were not in selling office space.

"His real bent is photography," wrote Bernard Wakefield, vice president of Cushman and Wakefield, in a letter of recommendation. "He is a natural artist in that line and is an extremely good all-around man with many interests."

A year later, Fenno's work came to the attention of *Fortune* magazine's art editor, who gave him his first magazine assignment—one that was followed by many more. By 1935, he was getting regular work and quit the real estate business.

Six years later, he had traveled as far as the Philippines and South America on assignments, working freelance, mostly for *Fortune,* though "practically every important periodical publication in the U.S. has used my photos at one time," he would later write.

But the fact of the matter was he had no degree and for that, he, too, would need a waiver to get into the Navy. Again, Steichen triumphed.

"Applicant has been interviewed and recommended by Lt. Cmdr. Edward John Steichen for a specific billet in the photographic department of the Aviation Training Department at the Bureau of Aeronautics," wrote Albert F.

Horace Bristol had lived abroad and was one of the earliest Life *magazine photographers. He already had books to his credit when he joined the Steichen unit.*

Rico, director of Naval Officer Procurement in New York, to the head of the Navy's personnel section at the Bureau of Navigation on March 10, 1942. "The applicant is considered outstanding in the photographic field so in view of these special qualifications, it is recommended that the lack of formal education be waived."

Jacobs, the former merchant deckhand, now had a set of Navy's lieutenant's bars and a spot in Steichen's unit.

"Taking photographs is something I like to do," he wrote. "What success I have had, and what reputation I may enjoy, is doubtless the result of that happy circumstance. It is not hard to do well at something you like to do."

Steichen's third recruit from the professional ranks was Horace Bristol, who brought the most photojournalism experience to the unit with his arrival in June of 1942.

Both his parents had worked in the newspaper industry. His father as a linotype operator at the *Los Angeles Times,* and his mother had a distinguished career as a reporter in Southern California before becoming women's editor at the *San Francisco Call-Bulletin,* quite an accomplishment for a woman in the 1930s.

Bristol attended the University of Southern California for a year, but dropped out when he injured his back playing football. He then attended the University of Redlands in the town of the same name east of Los Angeles while he recuperated from his injury.

His final attempt at college was at Stanford University, where he lasted a year before dropping out after receiving an inheritance from his grandfather.

After marrying his high school sweetheart, Virginia, he took off with his wife for Germany, where he again attempted college, this time in Munich, studying architecture.

Though he'd been exposed to photography through his father's job at the *Times,* he didn't buy a camera until he was living in Munich and only then as a tool to help him study buildings for his classes.

It was 1929 and Bristol had a front-row seat as Adolf Hitler rose to power in southern Germany, with copies of *Mein Kampf,* Hitler's autobiography, selling in all the store windows.

The crash of the stock market brought Bristol back to the United States, still without a college degree. Though the Depression considerably reduced his inheritance, he had enough money to bring his wife home and purchase a small weekly newspaper in the town of Piru, California, just north of Los Angeles in Ventura County.

By now, photography was his main interest, and while running the newspaper, he would drive forty-five miles to the Art Center School in Los Angeles to study under the noted Hollywood photographer Will Connell.

By 1933, Bristol had sold his newspaper and was trying, with some, but not much success, to make a living as a commercial photographer in Southern California.

Thinking things might be better elsewhere in the state, he moved his family north to San Francisco, where his mother was working at the *Call-Bulletin.*

It was here that his photographic career slowly took off. As the number of his commercial, newspaper, and magazine clients grew, he struck up friendships with the legendary Ansel Adams, whose studio was just a few doors down from Bristol's, the noted portrait artist Imogene Cunningham, and documentary photographer Dorothea Lange—all friendships that would last for decades.

His career took a giant step forward in 1936 when he started to work regularly for *Time* magazine and, just a year later, for *Life.* Bristol became one of that magazine's first staff photographers, with images in the inaugural issue.

In late 1937, he began to document the lives of migrant workers in the fields around San Francisco and pitched the idea of a *Life* magazine story to the editors, but was turned down flat by Wilson Hicks, the magazine's photo editor.

Undaunted, Bristol approached writer John Steinbeck about a book project on the subject and Steinbeck agreed, accompanying Bristol on several weekend trips into the migrant camps.

Bristol took hundreds of images of the workers and was sure there was a book in the offing, but Steinbeck abruptly pulled out of the project. He, too, saw a book in the stories of the workers the two had documented so heavily that year.

Steinbeck's book became the Pulitzer Prize–wining novel *The Grapes of Wrath,* while Bristol's images disappeared into history for nearly fifty years.

Stripped to the waist, Lieutenant Commander Horace Bristol works on Espiritu Santo in the New Hebrides Islands during operations in February 1944.

He continued working for *Life* during the next four years with assignments as far-ranging as native culture in the South Pacific island of Bali and the lumber industry in the Pacific Northwest.

Though no official record exists of just how Steichen came to offer Bristol a position in his unit, Bristol believed it was Tom Maloney of *U.S. Camera* who engineered the deal.

Like Jacobs, Bristol needed a waiver to enter the Navy because despite five-plus years of college, he didn't possess a degree. But based on his professional qualifications and the fact that he had more schooling than most college graduates, he obtained the waiver and, like Jacobs, was brought in as a lieutenant, reporting by late June of 1942 after six weeks of indoctrination training at Harvard University.

Meanwhile, Steichen was also recruiting others to work in a special photographic laboratory assembled in the Fisheries Building that sat on the National Mall not far from the Capitol. The Smithsonian Institution's National Air and Space Museum on Independence Avenue now occupies that ground.

The lab was designed by Leo Pavelle, who operated one of New York's best-known commercial photo laboratories at the start of World War II. The lab was more advanced than the rest of the Navy's labs and was even outfitted to handle the new Kodachrome film.

Pavelle was charged by Steichen to recruit young photographic technicians from the New York area. These experts were brought into the Navy as enlisted men who, after attending boot camp, would assume the ranks of third-, second-, or first-class photographic specialists—because they already had the training required by this position.

Sailors brought in by the mainstream photographic community, on the other hand, would attend the Navy's Photographic School in Pensacola, Florida, and then be designated photographer's mates.

Photographer's mates never quite accepted the photographic specialists as equals.

In February, Steichen contacted Ansel Adams, who himself was looking for a way to participate in the war effort.

"Adams, I want you to run my laboratory in Washington," Steichen said during a phone call to the photographer, who was then working at Yosemite, one of his favorite locations and one that won him lasting fame.

Adams told Steichen that he'd be delighted to come to work for him, despite a long-standing professional rivalry with the elder statesman of photography. Seems Adams was closer to Steiglitz in the photographic pecking order of the day and some of that rivalry had worn off on Adams.

But Adams was willing to put aside those differences to help in the war effort. Still, there was a catch: Adams told Steichen he would accept the position, but could not start until July 1, 1942, because of prior commitments. Steichen promised Adams he'd be in touch shortly.

"I waited for the promised call," Adams wrote in his autobiography. "After another month I read in a photographic magazine that Steichen had appointed someone else."

Adams was disappointed and his dislike for Steichen continued for the rest of his life.

One of Pavelle's recruits was young Marty Forscher, who would become the unit's camera repairman. He recalls exaggerating his qualifications in order to get a shot at the special unit.

"The Navy's official camera during World War II was the large and unwieldy Speed Graphic, which produced a four-by-five-inch negative," recalls Forscher, now a legendary repairman who was recruited as an apprentice repairman from the streets of New York.

Steichen, who had been experimenting with smaller handheld cameras just before the war, fought the Navy and, with Radford as his advocate, managed to get requisitions through the Navy supply channels for Leica, Rollieflex, and Kodak Medalist cameras.

"When Pavelle asked me if I had experience with these kinds of cameras," Forscher said, "of course I said I could work on anything—even though I had never even touched any of those cameras before."

Once through boot camp and working in Steichen's Washington lab, Forscher said he locked himself away in a room to learn each camera type.

"I would take them apart down to every last screw and put them back together," he recalled. "It took me three weeks to learn the Rollie, another three for the Leica and so on—but I learned them, every gear and every screw."

Forscher's hard work paid off and he soon became known by the unit's photographers as a miracle worker, someone who could repair gear considered to be damaged beyond all hope.

The initial crew wouldn't be complete until late 1942, when two other photographers joined the unit—Victor Hugo Jorgensen, the last officer photographer in the original crew, and Alfonso Iannelli, the unit's only enlisted photographer brought in by Steichen.

Along with Miller, Jorgensen was the least experienced of the photographers.

The tall and gangly native of Portland, Oregon, had also not completed college at the time he applied for entry into the Navy. Still, his records show he'd attended four full years, and only failed to complete his final examinations in the fall of 1933 because he'd already taken a job at his father's hotel in Portland.

A year later, he managed to get a job as an office boy at the *Portland Oregonian*.

A very young-looking Victor Jorgensen in one of his passport-style photos that were required as part of his application for a commission. The most inexperienced of the original crew, he was the only one brought in as an ensign—the lowest rank in the Navy's officer corps.

After only six months, he moved up to an apprentice reporter's position on the newspaper's information desk, which answered subscriber's questions.

Three months after that, he became a full reporter with a slot on the general reporting staff of the paper. It was then that he started to take an interest in photography.

"It was shortly after becoming a reporter that I began making use of pho-

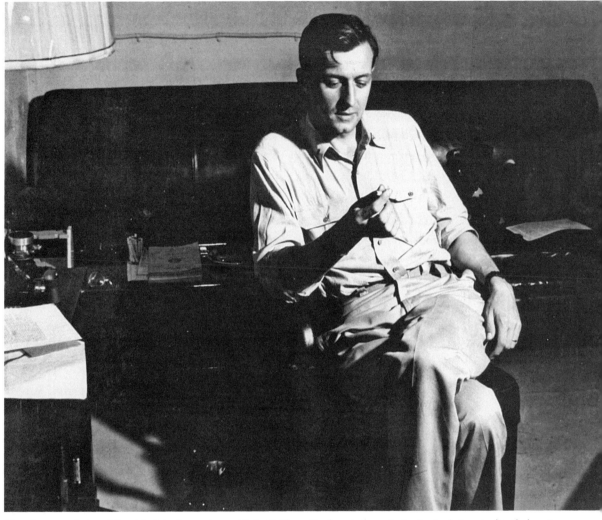

Victor Jorgensen, the last of the original six photographers to join the Steichen unit, relaxes in the carrier Lexington's *in-port cabin, the largest and most spacious living quarters on board the ship. Jorgensen was a writer and photographer for the* Portland Oregonian *before the war.*

tography in connection with reporting work," Jorgensen wrote in his Navy application. "In fact, my first 'front page' story included a layout of pictures that I had taken."

After that early success, he was often asked to fill in as a photographer when the regular staff was unavailable.

Though he continued to work for the paper as an editor in a special photographic section and later in the newspaper's Sunday magazine section, he also began to have some success as a freelance photographer. His work appeared in *Collier's,* the *Saturday Evening Post,* as well as in the *American Weekly* and even the *New York Times.*

Jorgensen's employer tolerated his freelance work, considering it professional development, as he was being groomed for a "major executive position," according to Edward M. Miller, acting managing editor of the paper in 1942, when Jorgensen was applying for his Navy commission.

But the young reporter and photographer had other ideas about where his career should go and learned in 1942 that Steichen was recruiting photographers for his special unit from State Senator Dick Newberger, whom Jorgensen knew from his newspaper job as a reporter and photographer.

Newberger was a friend of then Assistant Secretary of the Navy James Forrestal and heard about the Steichen unit from him.

"He wrote me a letter saying, why don't you make an application for it," Jorgensen recalled in a postwar interview. "The draft was breathing down my neck, so I said heck yes . . . And it worked out beautifully for me."

Though Steichen sought to bring in Jorgensen as a lieutenant, junior grade, the officer board balked at this and approved his application only as an ensign. The bump down didn't bother Jorgensen, who was just happy to be in uniform as a naval officer.

Soon he was off in Tucson, Arizona, going through his officer indoctrination, and almost ended up as an aviation maintenance officer until Steichen again intervened.

Before he graduated from his indoc course, the bureau ordered him to attend aviation maintenance officer school in Norman, Oklahoma, and then another school for photographic intelligence interpretation in Washington, D.C.

Getting wind of this, Steichen quickly had his contacts in the personnel section get the orders changed, sending Jorgensen directly to Washington and the Steichen unit in late February.

While Jorgensen was fighting his battles, Steichen was recruiting another young photographer, but since he had only one year of college, Steichen could only arrange for him to come in as a photographic specialist second class. The hope was to eventually get him a commission into the officer ranks.

His name was Alfonso Murello Iannelli. But he went by the name of Fons.

He had come to Steichen's attention through Pavelle, who had known Iannelli when the latter was the chief photographic illustrator for Tempo Incorporated, a large Chicago photo studio.

Iannelli was the son of Italian immigrants and his father was a well-known architect, artist, and sculptor who did work for Frank Lloyd Wright in the 1920s and 1930s.

Iannelli didn't have to go far when he enlisted on December 15, 1942, heading to the Great Lakes Naval Training Station near Waukegan, Illinois, for his basic training. After nearly nine weeks, he was transferred to Washington and went to work in the Fisheries Building for Steichen. Unlike the other enlisted men in the unit, he didn't stay in Washington long.

Sandburg's poetry and Steichen's edited photo selections were put together to visually show the American people that victory was possible because of the people of America. Steichen always believed that people were the basis of triumph.

Silence, yes.
Let them have silence.
Call the roll of their names
and let it go at that.
To long sleep and deep silence
they have gone.
Deep among the never forgotten.

BATAAN — CORREGIDOR

CHAPTER 3

The Road to Victory and the Home Front

★　　★　　★

THAT STEICHEN WAS the right man to oversee a documentary project on the Navy's role in the war would be proven over the coming years of conflict. But what is generally not known is that in order to become the right man for the job, he had to reinvent himself. Understanding this transformation is essential to understanding why Steichen at age sixty-two sought to make photography part of the war effort.

By 1938, Steichen was a legend. His style of portraiture was world renowned. His photos of the nation's stage and screen personalities and other famous faces, all made with eight-by-ten-inch view cameras and sheet film and with dramatic stagelike lighting, were instantly recognizable to readers of Condé Nast publications like *Vogue.*

Yet, despite the fact that his career was at its zenith, he decided he'd had enough and abruptly announced that he was closing his studio.

Many in the business thought this was an announcement of his retirement, and at the time Steichen did nothing to refute the idea. His autobiography, *A Life in Photography*, tells a different story.

"I was not closing my studio because I wanted to retire; after all, I was only 59," Steichen wrote. "I simply wanted to give myself a revitalizing change and move into new areas."

To Steichen, advertising work "had become more and more artificial," and fashion photography had become a routine to him. "The real fault was my own," he wrote. "I had lost interest because I no longer found the work challenging; it was too easy."

His departure from the advertising world was an event of some importance, and so, in January 1938, a crowd gathered for a farewell banquet at the Algonquin Hotel in midtown Manhattan.

Anyone who was anybody in the photographic and publishing worlds was in attendance. Most were his former clients and photographic friends such as Tom Maloney, editor and publisher of *U.S. Camera,* whom Steichen was working with even more closely than before. What no one realized on that night of his "retirement" was that the event marked the beginning of a new phase of his career.

Time magazine attempted to put Steichen's retirement into perspective for its readers. "If Chrysler were to retire from the auto industry, or Metro-Goldwyn-Mayer from the cinema," the magazine reported, "the event would be more surprising but no more interesting to either business than Steichen's was to his."

Noting the magnitude of the occasion, *Time* also seemed to laud him for his sudden exit, saying that Steichen's polished studio approach belonged to the photographic past and that his "love of lighting effects and studio magic" appeared to be "stagy."

In the view of *Time*'s editors, the future of the art belonged to younger photographers, the documentary-leaning photographers like Dorothea Lange, Walker Evans, Marion Post Wolcott, and Carl Mydans, who made up the cadre of their recently launched *Life* magazine.

Many of these photographers either had been or were currently employed by the Farm Security Administration, a division of the Department of Agriculture. The leader of this group was Roy Stryker, who was an agricultural educator turned photo editor.

Stryker's group had roamed the nation documenting the Depression with compelling, on-the-spot pictures to support the federal government's efforts to overcome the disastrous financial crisis of the era. The stark realism and candid nature of their style, enhanced by the use of smaller cameras and faster films, was a product of a less obtrusive working style than larger-format equipment permitted.

What *Time* saw was the passing of an era and predicted that Steichen's more artificial style of shooting would go with it. What the magazine didn't know was that even in his late fifties, Steichen yearned to learn more about the possibilities of photography and planned to expand his horizons by delving into documentary photography himself.

Thus, outfitted with the latest lightweight Contax 35mm camera and a stock of new Kodachrome film, Steichen traveled for two months to Mexico and the Yucatán. He wandered around, documenting the local life as he saw it, capturing images of Mexican children and colorfully dressed women going about their daily work. Though he would occasionally return to advertising and portrait work in the next few years, it was the use of the small cameras and the effort to delve deeply into subjects that would rule his future.

Steichen found himself captivated with the work of Stryker's Farm Security Administration photographers. On April 18, 1938, he attended the opening of the International Photographic Exposition at the Grand Central Palace in New York, which featured more than three thousand images produced by hundreds of photographers from around the world.

What caught Steichen's eye and influenced him greatly were the nearly seventy photographs from the FSA. "We scooped the show," Stryker wrote to a friend after the opening. "Even Steichen went to the show in a perfunctory manner and got a surprise when he ran into our section."

Steichen was so taken with the images that the 1938 version of Maloney's *U.S. Camera Annual* featured a large section of that unit's work. Steichen wrote the text that accompanied the images. The work, he wrote, was "a series of the most remarkable human documents that were ever rendered in pictures . . . these documents told stories, and told them with such simple and blunt directness that they made many a citizen wince."

Steichen saw that documentary photographs produced gut reactions in people and became a force for change. This human reaction to these pictures captivated him completely. It was one of the reasons that telling stories with images—lots of them—would come to take more and more of his attention.

He began taking more documentary photographs himself and also to orchestrate the work of others into the stories he told. In August 1941, with the United States on the threshold of all-out war, Steichen contributed to a special issue of *Fortune* magazine entitled "Total War for the U.S." His submission was a montage of images entitled "No Peace Without Power" and showed a terrified mother holding her child as bombs dropped from above juxtaposed with an image of a calm, pretty woman who held up her baby girl to the camera. In the background was a formation of U.S. warplanes and a caption that simply said "Buy Bonds Now."

A month later, just four months before Pearl Harbor, Steichen was approached by the Museum of Modern Art to produce a photo exhibit on national defense to be titled *The Arsenal of Democracy*. Steichen was hoping that he'd get in on the war as a member of the U.S. military, but the possibility seemed remote, so he saw this show as an alternative way to contribute to the war effort.

The exhibition marked the first time he was putting together a large show and he threw himself into its development with enthusiasim. After Pearl Harbor, the name of the project was changed to *The Road to Victory*. Though it still had the support of the Museum of Modern Art and was planned to open there, it was now under the auspices of the Office of War Information—giving Steichen more time and money to work with.

More than 90 percent of the images in the show came from agencies of the federal government and included pictures from Stryker's Farm Security Administration, the Army's Signal Corps, and, of course, Steichen's new employer, the Navy's Bureau of Aeronautics—after his miraculous entry into uniform had become a reality.

Though he was now in uniform, the Navy allowed Steichen to spend his first six months in the service editing the exhibition down from "tens of thousands of photographs" to a selection of 150 that would grace the museum's revamped second floor. He recruited his brother-in-law, the poet Carl Sandburg, to write the text for the show. Steichen wanted Sandburg's

simple words to guide the reader through the pictures, while not taking away from the impact of the images themselves.

He did not, it was widely noted, include any of his own images, a fact Steichen himself never explained. "Commander Steichen—perhaps the most celebrated living technician of the camera—has neither included any of his own photographs nor limited his choice of examples to those of technical excellence," the exhibition notes said. "Fascination with technical perfection has distracted many photographers and connoisseurs of photography from its chief natural function of documentation and human interest recording."

This would not be a standard gallery show of framed images lined up on walls. Instead, Steichen used a magazine-style layout. It was a style that would become his trademark, one he used again nearly fifteen years later when he produced the famous *Family of Man* exhibition at the same museum.

The whole second floor of the museum was redesigned to accommodate the layout, which guided visitors through the show. "Each room is a chapter, each photograph a sentence," said the notes to the show, whose subtitle would declare it to be "a procession of photographs of a nation at war." This symphony of photographs was not only hung on walls, but on the ceiling and the floor as well—juxtaposed for maximum impact by Steichen. Even the size of the images varied greatly and was part of Steichen's plan to get maximum impact, from the nearly standard eight-by-ten enlargement to murals that took up complete walls.

The visitor first saw Sandburg's simple words: "In the beginning was virgin land, and America was promises," with wall mural-size images of great Western canyons and California redwoods. In rapid succession, the viewer saw America's vast agricultural and industrial capabilities and the faces of the people from small towns and large cities.

OPPOSITE: *Newly minted Lieutenant Commander Edward Steichen and his brother-in-law, poet Carl Sandburg, discuss the layout of* The Road to Victory *exhibit at the Museum of Modern Art in New York City in early 1942.*

The show's dramatic high point, designed to infuse a sense of purpose in visitors, was in an alcove roughly halfway through the exhibition—a large image of the destroyer *Shaw* exploding at Pearl Harbor on December 7, 1941.

Underneath that huge image, Steichen placed a smaller image of Japanese Ambassador Nomura in a moment of hearty laughter with his "peace envoy" Kurusu. Those images were offset by another large mural, a Dorothea Lange photograph of a stern-looking Texas farmer standing against a sky of white clouds; the farmer's slightly squinting eyes are looking straight at the exploding *Shaw* and the words "War—they asked for it—now, by the living God, they'll get it" are the caption.

The exhibition's images of young American boys in Army training, on transport and other Navy ships, and images of groups of shiny war aircraft created still more drama. It concluded with photos of columns of marching American soldiers, while smaller panels pictured the reaction of proud fathers and beaming mothers and Sandburg's words proclaimed, "Tomorrow belongs to the children."

The exhibition opened to much fanfare on May 20, 1942. A private dinner was held in the museum's penthouse just before the doors were opened. Steichen showed up in his Navy dress blues as Lieutenant Commander Steichen, with his wife, Dana, at his side. The list of guests was a who's who of the photographic and publishing worlds and included Carl Sandburg and his wife, Lilian, Steichen's sister, along with publisher Condé Nast, Mrs. Simon Guggenheim, Roy Stryker, and the seventy-eight-year-old Alfred Steiglitz.

Steichen's plan for the show was to present America with an inspiring view of hope and potential. What the show proved to Steichen himself was that his talents in photography remained alive and vital in the new age of smaller cameras and documentary subjects. For Steichen, after months of hard work, this was a coming-out party for his second career; he was now back on top of the photographic world.

The show received rave reviews from the local press at a time when the outcome of the war seemed very much in doubt. The Japanese continued their

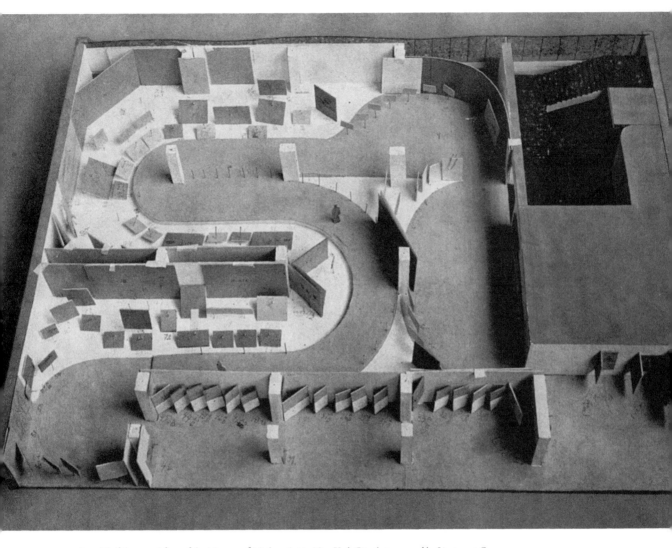

A model of the second floor of the Museum of Modern Art in New York City that was used by Lieutenant Commander Steichen and Mr. Herbert Bayer to plan out the location of every photograph used in the exhibit.

march across the Pacific and Hitler's forces were firmly in control of Europe. In this atmosphere, *The Road to Victory* was a symbol of the nation's resolve to fight back.

Steichen liked to use magazine-style layout in his positioning of photographs. By varying the size of individual images he could direct and guide the viewer to understand the message he was trying to portray.

"When his sense of drama is united to that possessed by the young men directing the shows in the modern museum, then indeed you get something terrific," wrote Henry McBride in the *New York Sun* on May 22. "The effect of these enormous photographs of war efforts with life-size portraits of typical citizens posed against them is overwhelming."

Even the communist newspaper the *Daily Worker* got on the bandwagon. "It's the most sensational exhibit that ever was shown in these parts; What a country to fight for!"

The climactic final layout of Steichen's exhibit showed America's military might in an effort to show the viewer that it was only a matter of time before the war would turn around and because of this, victory would be assured.

Ralph Steiner, the picture editor of PM, observed: "The photographs . . . have never been displayed before. They don't sit quietly on the wall. They jut out from the walls and up from the floors to assault your vision."

The *New York Times*'s Edwin Alden Jewell, chimed in on May 22. "The drama enacted transcends the picturing of a nation at war, in that it searches and searchingly reveals the very fiber of the nation that is now fighting to preserve all it holds most dear . . . in its vast sum it constitutes a true, a stirringly articulate portrait of America." It was the emotions the show brought out in people that Jewell said made it a must see for all Americans. "It would not at all amaze me to see people, even people who have thought themselves very worldly, nonchalant, or hard-boiled, leave this exhibition with brimming eyes."

The fashion giant, *Vogue*, told its readers that the "world is crowding" to the Museum of Modern Art.

During the next six months 80,000 visitors saw the exhibition in New York, though it did not stop there. *The Road to Victory* went on the road, too, making stops in Cleveland, Chicago, St. Louis, Rochester, and Portland, Oregon. Smaller versions were shipped to Honolulu, Columbia, and Uruguay as well as England. Ironically, the cargo ship taking the exhibition to the United Kingdom was torpedoed and sunk by a German submarine, and a replacement version had to be produced. It made it through on the second try.

The exhibition was also set up at embarkation points and shown to U.S. troops as they prepared to board troop ships and head off to war zones and small, pocket versions were also distributed to the troops as well. Asked by *Newsweek* to account for the overwhelming popular reaction, Steichen said, "It shows the good common horse sense of the common people, it will give them something to base their faith upon."

But Steichen's images moved American photography into another realm. *The Road to Victory* contributed significantly to photography's entrance into a new area, one that both sides in the war would seek to exploit on a regular basis—propaganda.

Documentary photography in American had it's roots in a vehicle for social change. Now it moved on as a vehicle for the United States government to assist the nation to mobilize to meet a world threat. This caused some concerns in American photographic circles. Some, including Nancy Newhall, the wife of MOMA's photo curator Beaumont Newhall, panned the exhibition as sentimental, though this was clearly a minority view in a country that was already on a wartime footing.

Steichen's transformation from the top advertising photographer in the nation to a force in documentary journalism was complete, validated by the success of *The Road to Victory*. He was now ready to turn his energies elsewhere, though he would return again and again to the exhibition format to show-case the work of his photographers both inside and outside the Navy.

With the show up and running, Steichen and Dana pulled up stakes in Connecticut and New York and moved into a rented townhouse in Washington, D.C.'s Georgetown neighborhood, not far from the downtown government office buildings where his unit was forming up.

Once in Washington, Steichen started on a schedule of twelve-hour days. Though he was now sixty-three years old, he reveled in the new challenge and his boundless energy amazed those more than half his age. By early June he had three photographers onboard and others on the way. Wasting no time, Steichen began to plan extended travel for unit members to document Navy aviation training. His ultimate goal was to document the war but he decided that would have to come later.

CHAPTER 4

1942:
Early Days and a Taste of War

★   ★   ★

STEICHEN ARRIVED IN Washington in late May 1942 flush with the success of *The Road to Victory.* Having met one challenge, he had another awaiting him, and he was primed and ready to get the unit off the ground and get his photographers, himself included, out shooting pictures.

He rented a town house in the Georgetown area for himself and Dana and started to work just a few miles away at the unit's offices in the Fisheries Building.

Just days after Steichen's arrival, on June 1, Charles Kerlee, the first photographer, reported for duty.

Charles Fenno Jacobs arrived on June 5, just in time to head south with Steichen and Kerlee. Horace Bristol joined them on the road a few days later.

While Steichen had been in New York preparing *The Road to Victory*, the Navy had been holding the line against the Japanese in the Pacific at the costly Battle of the Coral Sea.

Lieutenant Wayne Miller, the unit's first member, said his first few months in the unit, waiting for Steichen to arrive, were ones he'd like to forget. Though he'd been sprung from his job in the classified material vault, he ended up simply watching as the Steichen unit came together.

PREVIOUS PAGE: *Ordnance sailors check belts of .50-caliber ammunition on the deck of the escort carrier* Santee *before loading them into aircraft preparing to launch.*

He was not an active participant yet, though he did spend some time organizing the offices and ordering much of the basic equipment and supplies the photographers would need once they started work.

"For those first weeks and months I basically did nothing and Steichen really gave me no guidance or instruction on anything to do, either," Miller recalls. "I just sat around with nothing to do except order supplies and, oh yeah, answer the telephone."

Steichen had just arrived in Washington when the crucial Battle of Midway was fought over three days in early June 1942—ironically coinciding with the unit's first road trip.

But even with the headlines talking about a naval action in the Pacific, Steichen and his men did not head to war; for the moment, their job was to document sailors and naval aviation training around the country.

Steichen's early battles were mostly with the Navy's brass about the role of his photographers. He wanted them to work in uniform as they had worked in civilian life—as freewheeling freelancers—a concept unheard of in the Navy's rigid bureaucracy. Officers just didn't carry cameras—or any luggage, for that matter.

"I soon found out that we were a rather irregular unit in the organizational setup in the Navy, and at first, we met with opposition from the Navy's regular photographic service," Steichen would write later.

According to Miller, the only thing that saved the unit from being absorbed into the regular Navy photographic community—and possibly disbanded—was that it was tucked away in the Bureau of Aeronautics, a special unit in the training-literature department and not a part of the Navy's photographic bureaucracy.

"Steichen knew the importance of this, as in the early days of the war it was all about training—that's where the money and resources were, and he could pretty much get whatever he wanted if he could convince his bosses it was necessary for training," Miller said.

This relative cloistering of the team kept him out of the line of fire from the

Navy's traditional photographer's mates and photographic officers who didn't see the need for Steichen's crew.

The old man had recruited his photographers by promising them carte blanche in their photographic ventures. He'd successfully argued with Radford that his shooters must be officers and now he had to deliver on his promises of outstanding images.

Already in uniform for five months, Steichen was feeling pressure to produce results as quickly as possible. As a result, the "old man" and his photographers in the Training and Literature Field Unit #1, as they were officially called, prepared to start documenting aviation training.

Kerlee and Jacobs had no time to get settled in Washington. In fact, though officially based there during the war, first out of the Navy's Bureau of Aeronautics and later as a unit directly assigned to the staff of the chief of naval operations, the group would spend few days in D.C. over the next three years.

But now the adventure was young and the photographers would begin to create the images that were their initial mission—to promote naval aviation outside the service and provide images for the plethora of training publications and posters and other media the service would need as it ramped up the military training machine.

"I was anxious to get to Washington, and to work, as there was so much to do," Steichen would write years later. Once in the capital city, he set a brutal pace. He was up at 6:30 am, his wife Dana would recall, and he routinely put in twelve-hour days at the office before heading home and to bed by nine-thirty—a schedule he sometimes kept up seven days a week throughout the war.

His first project was creating plans to circle the country and photograph activities at six different naval air stations and other installations. The trip was to take over a month and would take the unit to more than fifteen major cities and along nearly all of the nation's coastlines.

During and after this trip, Steichen learned just how difficult traveling with Navy orders could be. This became painfully obvious when he tried to get Kerlee's orders modified en route to allow him to stop for a few days at the

Rear Admiral John S. McCain commanded aircraft carriers before he became head of the Bureau of Aeronautics in 1942, replacing then-Captain and later Admiral Radford as Steichen's boss. It was portraits like this brooding one of McCain that were very much in the style he used for celebrities when he captured their images for Vanity Fair *in the '20s and '30s—a style he continued when he photographed the Navy brass. Steichen would hold portrait sittings in Washington and later in Pearl Harbor and would be swamped by officers wanting to be photographed by the "Great Steichen."*

Navy's Training Station in Chicago, and at the same time to get Jacobs's orders modified to allow him to head to New York City to get the images processed. At this early stage, Steichen's custom lab in the Fisheries Building was not yet completed.

It would be a lesson he took to heart and sought to fix.

Because their orders were set in stone in Washington, and their itinerary strict, it took another mountain of paperwork, memos, and phone calls to get the officers' orders straightened out so they would be reimbursed for their travel and expenses once they returned to the capital.

With Radford's help and that of higher-ups in the Navy Department, Steichen arranged with the Navy's personnel officials, then housed in what was called the Bureau of Navigation, to provide his men with special orders that were written in vague enough language to allow them the flexibility he wanted.

Best of all, Steichen set up the system so his photographers could plan their own trips and submit their own paperwork to get their orders cut without higher approval.

"Once we learned how to do this, we were set," said Lieutenant Victor Jorgensen, who showed up in December of 1942 just as the unit was beginning to gather steam within the Navy Department. "It was just unreal what kind of access that gave us—and the eyebrows it raised, too."

Lieutenant Barrett Gallagher, who would join the unit in late 1944, claims the orders had the ability to evoke strange responses from those who read them, as they authorized the photographers not only total freedom of movement but also to have two hundred pounds of excess baggage, and the priority to bump many senior officers off flights.

"That didn't go over too well with some senior officers," Gallagher would recall. "No one wants to give up their seat, but to have it go to someone junior in rank did not make us too popular with some."

As Gallagher prepared to make his inaugural trip as part of the unit in November 1944, he made his way with all his gear from New York to Treasure Island in San Francisco, and from there was trying to get on a booked-solid Navy PBY Catalina seaplane bound for Pearl Harbor.

As he was only a lieutenant at the time, he presented his orders to another Navy lieutenant who was manning the transportation desk at the flight terminal.

"He told me the flight was full and I should get used to the idea of waiting for the next flight, which had not yet been scheduled and I encouraged him to read my orders carefully before he made any final decisions," he said. "He studied those orders carefully, pausing occasionally to look up at me and my rank and look back to the paper—he did this several times."

Finally the officer stopped and looked at Lieutenant Gallagher with a puzzled face and declared, "Who the hell are you anyway, Jesus Christ? I have been manning this desk for a long time now, but I've never seen orders like these at all."

Gallagher made the flight, leaving a Navy captain confused and disgruntled at how a junior officer could have received such high-powered orders.

He encountered similar reactions when he arrived in the Pacific. Gallagher had heard from the other unit members that the best course of action was to get attached temporarily to an admiral's staff while on ships and under way.

"This would accomplish a few things right off the bat," Gallagher said. "It would guarantee you a rack and a laundry ticket, but most of all it kept you from having to stand long boring watches—that's because junior officers, once on board ship, were looked upon as free labor and assigned to various duties and watches—but no one dared mess with those assigned to the flag staff."

Such was the case for Gallagher as he reported on board the aircraft carrier *Intrepid,* then the flagship of Rear Admiral Gerald Bogan, with his vaunted orders in hand.

"Once onboard, I first asked to see Bogan and then I asked him personally to join his staff," Gallagher said.

"Son, what do your orders say?" Bogan asked, sizing up the brash young lieutenant and photographer in front of him.

BACKGROUND PHOTO: *Striking Back. November 8, 1943, flying in the back of a TBF Avenger aircraft, Bristol documents the first landing of U.S. troops on the North African shore.*

"Sir, my orders are to go wherever I want, stay as long as I want and to return home when I feel like it," Gallagher recalled saying as he handed his paperwork to the man wearing a single admiral's star on his collar—royalty in Navy circles.

"Well, boy, why don't you go and get something to eat and come and see me when I've had the time to read these amazing orders," Bogan said.

When he returned later, Gallagher was greeted by the now-amazed admiral in his stateroom and braced himself for a butt chewing for his behavior.

"Son, I'll be dammed if your orders aren't exactly as you stated," Bogan said, getting up from a chair and extending his hand to the photographer. "Welcome to my staff!" he said while shaking Gallagher's hand.

"I was with him the rest of the war, just like that," Gallagher would recount in years later. "He never gave me an order; I never had any conflict with him, but anywhere I went in the Navy, to any ship or anyplace in the Navy, all I had to was say 'Bogan sent me' and it was much better than any orders—it was the 'open sesame' to the whole thing for me."

It was a relationship that would not only last the war, but for the remainder of the two men's lives, as Gallagher would continue to cover the Navy well into the 1970s.

By the time Gallagher joined the unit, the way had been paved by other unit members for over a year. But as Steichen and the others headed out for their multicity training base tour in 1942, they were about to tread in uncharted waters.

"The Navy's culture didn't allow for officers to carry their own baggage before the war," Steichen said. "It just wasn't done in the days before the war, but here we were, three officers showing up with cameras over our shoulders, we were initially met with resistance from the 'regular Navy' officers."

But after Steichen simply made a call to Washington, Radford sent out another message to all the base and unit commanders to leave him and his men alone to do their job. The issue never came up again outside of Washington.

Though he often needed Radford's assistance to "grease the skids" outside of Washington, Steichen's own name was often enough for him to gain access to many of the Navy's top admirals in the capital.

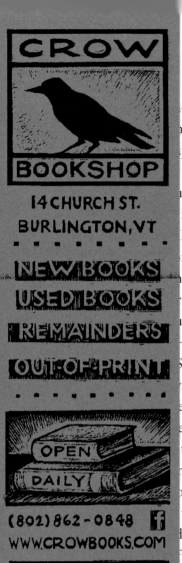
...otographer led many of the brass and civilian leadership in
...him out to "get their picture taken by the great Steichen."
...pher immediately saw the benefit of dusting off his old
... skills and used his abilities to shoot portraits of anyone of
...ld help him.

...in other military services, there exists a system by which
...ly scratched for favors. A captain, admiral, or civilian
...re likely to help Steichen gain access to a remote base or
...is control if he had a photo of himself taken by Steichen
...e in his home or office.

...mshaw"—taken from a Xiamen Chinese word that means
...—and it has come to mean getting something through
...Steichen just called it good business, and often his photog-
...ith stacks of photographs of ships and aircraft to give out
...ed them.

...ere not the usual stuffy portraits produced by Navy photo
...the subject impeccably dressed, seated in a chair with his
...t of him, and looking like he had a board nailed to his back.
...ortraits have survived, and some can even be found hang-
...today.

...dmiral Louis Denfield, who eventually became the chief of
...ter the war, was the Navy's top personnel admiral in 1942.
...phed him in dramatic *Vanity Fair* style standing in front of
... with his right hand inside his coat pocket—thumb and
...de to keep his hand from disappearing into the cloth.

The photograph still graces the walls outside the office of the Navy's current chief of personnel at the Arlington Annex in Arlington, Virginia. Its
style stands in such stark contrast to the official Navy portraits of other admirals that people often stop to admire it.

Being known in Washington also helped Steichen keep his officers out of
hot water. Such was the experience Jorgensen had with then Chief of Naval
Operations Ernest J. King, the Navy's top admiral.

Rear Admiral Louis Denfield, then the Navy's chief of the Bureau of Navigation—later renamed the Bureau of Personnel—worked with Steichen to give his men orders that would allow freedom of movement throughout the United States and eventually the war theaters. This portrait of Denfield still hangs outside the office of the chief of naval personnel in Arlington, Virginia.

"I was over in the Navy Department, on some sort of job and trotting down one of those mile-long corridors with both hands full of gear," he recounted. "And who comes steaming down the corridor but the King himself—E. Jesus King!

"So what do I do, my hands are full and I can't salute him—I should have dropped everything and snapped to attention, but I didn't."

Instead Jorgensen kept going right on by the admiral and his entourage, saying "howdy do, Admiral, nice day," as he passed.

"One of his coterie peeled off and came alongside me asking me my name and unit," he said. "I guess Steichen got a little read off for that because that was strictly not done in the Navy—but we got away with it one way or another."

But all that was in the future as Steichen left from Washington's Union Station with Miller, Kerlee, and Jacobs in tow, and boarded a train heading south to Jacksonville, Florida, the first stop on a five-week, sixteen-city tour, shooting everything they could get access to. Bristol would join them five days later in Pensacola.

Miller recalled waking up the first morning in the top berth of a sleeper car and peering over the side to see Steichen groping around, trying to find his glasses.

"This man was sixty-two years old, he'd been in World War I and was a legend in his field, why did he want to go to war again?" Miller recalled. "He absolutely amazed all of us with his energy and stamina."

While in Miami on June 7, the group got news of the Navy's first victory of the war—the Japanese fleet had been met at Midway and in a decisive three-day battle had been turned back to Japan.

Buoyed by the news, Steichen set a brutal pace on the road that was just as tough as his office schedule, and his boundless energy left his young photographers in the dust.

The first time Jorgensen met Steichen in person was on the road. The young lieutenant had been ordered down to Jacksonville Naval Air Station to meet up with Steichen and Kerlee.

"I don't remember what the name of the hotel was, but there he was, you

Aviation cadets await training flight hops in ready room at Kingsville Field, Naval Air Training Center, Corpus Christi, Texas.

couldn't miss him," Jorgensen said. "He was sixty-two, or something like that, but he had more energy than the rest of us put together.

"When I got there, poor Kerlee had been run right down to the knees. [Steichen] ran me ragged. For sixty-two he had fabulous energy—he could go eighteen hours a day, dead flat out and he'd do it more often than not."

The unit's early photos are scattered throughout the National Archives collection and it requires a hunt to find them. Steichen's crew not only photographed ground activities at the stations, but flew in aircraft, producing many images of the Navy's inventory of aircraft images for training.

Many of these early images are strictly documentary in style, capturing young sailors working on aircraft, launching, and recovering. Though each of the photographers would move over this ground time and time again over the next year and produce more in-depth and interesting imagery, some of this early work was very assembly-line looking.

What Steichen was doing here was building a library of aviation photographs that could be used for anything from Navy magazines and manuals to public release. The members of the unit documented any type of aircraft they could see and any kind of activity that presented itself in the short span of time, sometimes only one day, they shot at each station.

Some memorable images presented themselves on the journey. In San Diego in late June, Steichen photographed lines of sailors, with their seabags and hammocks lashed together and perched on their shoulders, walking single file to their new ships as others sit and read and watch.

But the visual skill of the photographers Steichen had picked is evident as many of the images of these early training days are beautifully lit with multiple flashbulbs—in many cases, making it look like the pictures was shot in natural light. This was particularly evident in Kerlee's photos of a group of sailors learning to maintain aircraft engines at the Navy pier in Chicago.

Some of the work rivaled the best magazine photographs of the day. But as a group, this early work displayed little imagination and was not well captioned; for the most part, the identities of the photographers are not known. The work pales in comparison to the images that were to come.

Though the photos show a technical purity, their subject matter was

Aviation cadets check flightboards for last-minute instructions at Naval Air Training Center, Corpus Christi, Texas, in October 1942.

repetitious at best. This was probably by design, as Steichen was trying to build up a mass of images and show his superiors he could deliver what he promised.

For the rest of 1942, Steichen stayed in Washington, tending to administrative duties and working to get the unit firmly rooted in the Bureau of Aeronautics—and out of the prying hands of the Navy's regular photographic hierarchy, which never ceased trying to shut Steichen and his unit down or at least absorb them into their world, where they could then keep them under control.

Meanwhile, Miller, Kerlee, Bristol, and Jacobs continued to visit and revisit bases up and down the East and Gulf coasts. Here, each began his flying career, making beautiful images of every type of Navy aircraft in the air, alone and in formations—including the Navy's hotter-than-air dirigibles in Lakehurst, New Jersey.

Miller would visit many of the Navy's preflight training bases set up at colleges around the country, giving new pilots their first taste of Navy life in a boot-camp environment. He also got a firsthand look at Marine aviation in South Carolina, including an exclusive look at Marine parachute and glider training.

Many of these images made it into the press in short order. *U.S. Camera,* for example, ran a large feature on the unit and its early work in early 1943.

It was during such a routine trip to Norfolk in the fall of 1942 that Horace Bristol began to make friends with members of a fighter squadron, VGF-29. "VGF" is Navy shorthand for an escort fighter squadron.

He spent weeks photographing the unit as they learned their craft, practicing their carrier takeoffs and landings first at a remote airfield in Virginia Beach, away from the prying eyes of the public, and later at sea on the escort carrier *Charger,* operating in the Chesapeake Bay.

The cities of Norfolk and Virginia Beach were all abuzz with rumors of an impending Allied invasion of Europe. Something was definitely in the air, but it was an invasion of North Africa, not Europe, though no one knew this at the time.

Bristol made good friends with the squadron's commanding officer, Lieutenant Commander Charles Blackburn, who would remain a friend of the Steichen unit throughout the war.

A 1933 Naval Academy graduate, Blackburn had been a young lieutenant teaching flying near Miami when he got tapped to lead the escort fighter unit a few months into the war.

At Blackburn's urging, Bristol approached Steichen about joining the squadron at sea. It was the opening Steichen was looking for, a chance for his boys to show their mettle in a real operation—something that counted.

Steichen agreed to the idea and Bristol returned to Norfolk, joining the squadron as their aircraft were craned on board their new home—a 559-

foot-long and 75-foot-wide escort carrier called the *Santee*. The larger carriers of the day were 300 feet longer and 30 feet wider on average.

At the time, the U.S. Navy, however, was short of carriers, the *Lexington, Yorktown,* and *Wasp* having already been sunk by the Japanese; the *Hornet* would follow them to the bottom within the month. This left the nation with only the *Saratoga, Enterprise,* and *Ranger* as top-of-the-line carriers.

Until the Navy finished building the newer, Essex-class carriers under construction at the time, the "jeep" carriers, as the escorts were sometimes called, would have to handle the load.

Built and commissioned as a fleet oiler in 1940, the *Santee* entered Norfolk Naval Shipyard in the spring of 1942 for conversion to a carrier. The work was done in just over four months; the ship was recommissioned as a carrier on August 24 and began her sea trials with shipyard workers still on board.

A flight of TBF Avenger torpedo bombers during a training flight over the Atlantic during training operations in September 1942.

Bristol was not on board September 24, when the first aircraft landed on the ship's flight deck, but reported aboard October 6, when the ship left for Bermuda to finish her shakedown period.

Carrier life is one of routine punctuated by moments of sheer terror. As the escort for many transports and surface combat ships en route to Africa for the Allies' first invasion of enemy territory, the *Santee* was engaged in antisubmarine warfare, and her aircraft flew many missions searching for German submarines.

Bristol flew almost daily as part of these patrols, racking up over twenty-

An SBD Dauntless dive-bomber gets the "wave off" from the landing signal officer on the deck below during an attempted landing on the deck of an aircraft carrier during the invasion of North Africa.

A flight deck crewman checks the wheel chocks of an aircraft secured to the deck of the escort carrier Santee *during the Atlantic passage as the ship made its way to the North African coast for the first Allied invasion of the war.*

six hours of flight time and producing beautiful images of the *Santee* and the other ships of the task group as well as stunning images of aircraft in formation and alone over the group.

During these operations, Bristol got a firsthand taste of the dangers of flight-deck life on October 30, when an SBD dive-bomber being launched from the ship's catapult lost its five-hundred-pound bomb on takeoff. The bomb had been fitted for hunting submarines and was set to detonate underwater.

The horrified crew thought they were home free once the bomb rolled diagonally off the port side of the flight deck and into the water. But seconds later, it detonated, rocking the ship so heavily that the radars were damaged and the homing device pilots used to guide themselves back to the carrier into the water was knocked out.

The accident was the only departure from routine during the transit. But the lack of a homing device would later become a problem for Bristol's new-found friend, Blackburn, and the fighter squadron.

Most of the time when he was not flying, Bristol worked the flight deck, photographing aircraft launches and recoveries as well as maintenance activities. Soon, though, boredom set in and he began to look for other aspects of life on the *Santee* to document.

Bristol produced a series of images of Lieutenant Brinkley Bass, Blackburn's executive officer, laughing while getting his hair cut. Bass was already a recipient of two Navy Cross medals for his heroism in single-handedly sinking a Japanese warship and for taking a leading part in the sinking of a

BACKGROUND: *Containing men and machines of the U.S. Army, a convoy of ships makes its way across the Atlantic for the invasion of North Africa.*

Japanese carrier during the Battle of the Coral Sea—while his own carrier, the first USS *Lexington* was being sunk itself.

At sea, water can be scarce and the normally rigid personal grooming standards of the Navy sometimes are set aside for practical purposes. Sailors often grow beards and this fact fascinated Bristol.

He made portraits of more than fifty officers and enlisted sailors who grew beards during the voyage. Some were simple portraits of their faces, others were head-and-shoulders "environmental portraits," while still others were shot as the men were doing their jobs.

A flight of SBD Daunt-less dive-bombers passes over a Navy destroyer during operations in the Atlantic during training operations in September 1942. The aircraft are from the escort carrier Santee, *which was in training for the invasion of North Africa.*

The captions of the images had one thing in common; they mentioned the fact that the subject had a beard.

On November 7, the *Santee* arrived with the invasion force off French Morocco and Bristol was up flying in a predawn launch the next morning in the back of a torpedo bomber, producing high-altitude images of the first landing craft making their way to the enemy beaches just after first light.

Blackburn's fighters had been given orders to strafe an airfield near the town of Safi, but they soon discovered that the base didn't exist. Looking for other targets, they circled the area for a while, as there was little or no anti-aircraft fire. Tired and frustrated, the aviators turned back to the carrier, but the weather had become rainy and the visibility went down to almost zero.

Opposite: *A chief petty officer (right) and junior sailor do maintenance on torpedoes in their storage magazine belowdecks on the escort carrier* Santee.

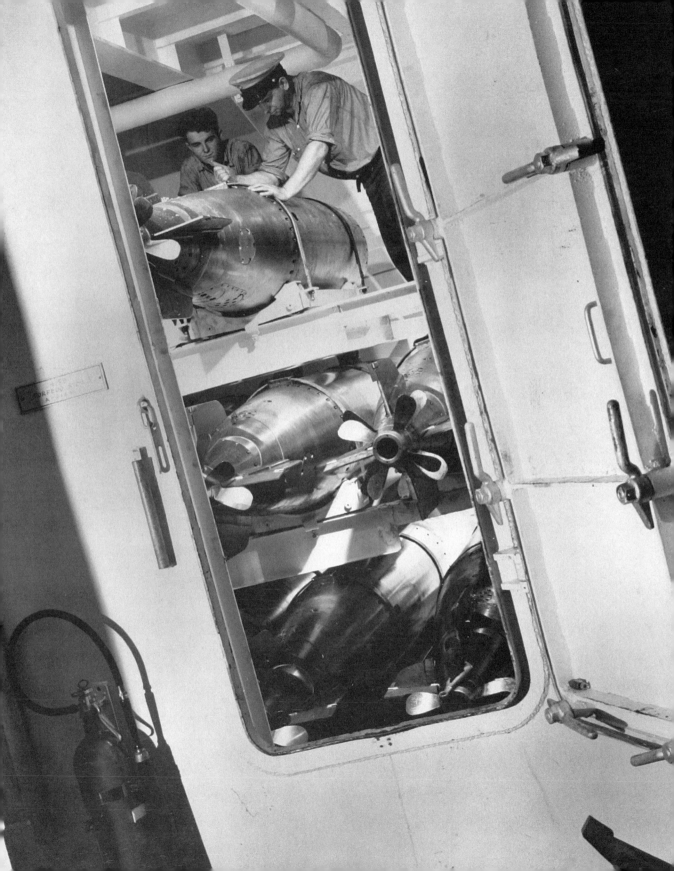

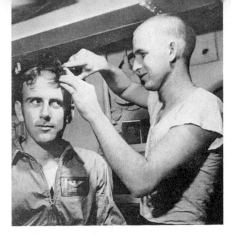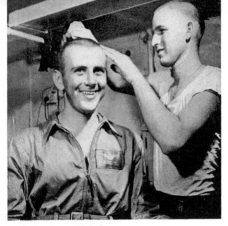

Lieutenant Brinkley Bass, a fighter pilot in Fighter Squadron 29 on-board the escort carrier Santee, *had twice been awarded the Navy Cross while flying off the carrier* Lexington *during the Battle of the Coral Sea in early 1942. Here, Horace Bristol captures Bass having his head shaved prior to launching in his aircraft for the invasion of North Africa.*

After working to find the ship by conventional means, Blackburn attempted to locate it by using a standard radio signal. Low on fuel, he sent the rest of his fighters back to land while he used the last of his fuel in a vain attempt to locate the ship and guide in his squadron mates.

He ditched his Wildcat in the ocean, tossed aside his unused parachute, and took to his small life raft. For three days he drifted, figuring the current was taking him toward land, but that it would take six or more days to reach it.

His luck changed on the third day when a task force steamed right toward him and he was picked up by one of the group's destroyers, which transferred him back on board the *Santee* dangling in a canvas bag suspended from a wire stretched between the two ships. Bristol caught the moment on film as well as the squadron leader's first minutes back on board the ship.

Bristol's flight, too, had difficulty making it back to the ship on the eighth, but somehow his pilot found the ship and made a landing—one of the few aircraft that returned that first day. Bristol returned to the air the next three days, producing aerial reconnaissance photos for intelligence purposes.

By November 22, the *Santee,* with Bristol on board, arrived back in Norfolk, and the photographer, with film in hand, drove back to find an eager Steichen. The images he'd produced caused quite a positive stir in the Navy Department and Bristol and Steichen got much attention from the brass as a result.

Bristol's photographs from the mission were given wide play in military and civilian magazines, and one image, taken from the island superstructure of the

OPPOSITE: *Sailors of a beaching crew prepare to bring ashore a P2Y flying boat during training operations at Naval Air Station, Norfolk.*

The National Ensign flies over F4F aircraft as it prepares to take off from the deck of the escort carrier Santee. *This photo was one of Bristol's most famous from the war and got wide play nationwide and was often mimicked by others.*

Santee, showed an American flag flapping in the breeze, framing aircraft that were preparing to take off from the deck below; behind the ship, following close in its wake, was a Navy destroyer. Another image, of *Santee* crew members doing jumping jacks on the ship's flight deck, silhouetted against the morning sky, would sit on Steichen's office wall during the war.

The photo was widely acclaimed as a symbol of the nation gathering strength and gave millions who saw it hope, Steichen would write later. But though Bristol received recognition inside the Navy for his work on the *Santee,* none of the millions of Americans who saw his photos had any idea who had shot them.

It was the one battle Steichen lost and would continue to lose during the war. Navy tradition was to identify photographs as "Official U.S. Navy Photograph," but not the photographer.

This frustrated the Steichen unit photographers to no end. Their civilian peers covering the same war were gaining attention since their names accompanied their images into all the major publications.

Throughout the war, Steichen continually lobbied the Navy's leadership to change this practice, but was unsuccessful each time. But though "officially released" images did not carry photographers' names, Steichen's own captions for his unit's images always identified who shot them—information that lives on today in the National Archives collections.

Nevertheless, Bristol's three weeks at war had gained the unit a reputation and the popularity of the work clearly demonstrated the value of the unit and the officer photographers who were a part of it.

Lieutenant Commander Tom Blackburn, then-commanding officer of Fighter Squadron 29 on board the escort carrier Santee, *transfers by breeches buoy from a tanker back to the USS San-tee after spending sixty-four hours in the ocean waiting for rescue during the invasion of North Africa in November 1942.*

Crewmembers of the escort carrier Santee *do morning exercises on the flight deck. This Bristol photograph was one that Steichen was quite fond of, and he kept a copy of it on the wall of his office throughout the war.*

An enlisted Navy photographer caught during an off moment at Naval Air Station Seattle during the first trip by the Steichen unit to numerous bases around the nation.

Aviation officer candidates in preflight training at Naval Air Station, Seattle, Washington, learn to march and carry weapons while being conditioned and screened for flight duty in July 1942.

Ordnancemen loading ammunition into belts to be loaded onto aircraft at Naval Air Station, Norfolk, Virginia.

A crewmember climbs up an accommodation ladder into the fuselage of a Navy aircraft at Naval Air Station, San Diego, California, in August 1942.

Ordnancemen crank a torpedo into place on the wing of a PBY Catalina aircraft during training operations at Naval Air Station, Jacksonville, Florida, in July 1942.

Aviation electricians' mates work inside an aircraft undergoing maintenance at Naval Air Station, Norfolk, Virginia, in September 1942.

Mess stewards relaxing in their berthing compartment on board the carrier Saratoga *by playing card games. Lieutenant Wayne Miller spent much time documenting the* Saratoga *belowdecks in November 1944, especially the stewards who at the time were considered second-class citizens in the Navy.*

CHAPTER 5

1943:
WAVES and the Pacific Offensive

STEICHEN'S UNIT WAS just beginning to show the Navy what it could do as the United States moved into its second full year in the war.

Though Bristol had seen action in North Africa, most of the unit was still documenting training operations as 1942 came to a close. This would gradually change over the next twelve months.

In early 1943, *U.S. Camera* magazine ran a spread of the unit's photographs and an article detailing the work and techniques of the photographers, but for security reasons did not mention any of their names.

Illustrating the article were Bristol's images from the *Santee* in North Africa, Steichen's and Bristol's work with aviation training in Florida, as well as Ensign Wayne Miller's work at Parris Island, South Carolina, documenting the early days of the Paramarines learning to be parachute-dropped.

Lieutenant Charles Kerlee would be next to get a taste of war zones on board the auxiliary carrier *Suwannee,* which was fresh from the North Africa landings and being fitted out for the Pacific, where it was expected to see more action.

The *Suwannee*'s skipper, Captain Jocko Clark, had seen Horace Bristol in action firsthand and was more than willing to take along another member of Steichen's unit.

Leaving on December 5, 1942, from Norfolk, the ship cleared the Panama Canal on December 12 and arrived in New Caledonia on January 4, 1943. Kerlee would spend the next six days on the ship, flying with aircrews providing escort to Navy and merchant vessels in and around the Solomon Islands, including support to the

Marines on Guadalcanal, but he didn't see any significant action during his short stay and was back in Washington by the end of January.

Wayne Miller finally set foot on a Navy ship just as 1942 came to a close. His first taste of steel decks under his feet wasn't on the high seas; instead, it was on an ad hoc aircraft carrier operating on Lake Michigan out of Chicago. Hardly the high-seas adventure he was looking for; that would come later in 1943 and was almost more than he bargained for.

Miller had been sent to shoot a story on the training carrier *Wolverine,* the Navy's first training aircraft carrier, which started life in 1913 as a sidewheel excursion steamer. Acquired by the Navy in March of 1942, she was fitted with a 550-foot flight deck and commissioned in August with one mission—to be a large training aid for pilots learning to put down an aircraft on a rolling flight deck.

The Navy would eventually operate two of these ad hoc flattops during the war, training thousands of pilots in the safety of the Great Lakes and freeing up operational carriers for wartime service.

Miller spent two days on board photographing student pilots who would fly out of Naval Air Station Glenview. Though the ship had a flight deck, it did not have elevators or a hangar deck, so student pilots had to land and take aircraft off as quickly as possible—a single student miscue that kept an aircraft on board would stop operations until that aircraft could either take off or be craned off back in Chicago.

Miller photographed the student pilots practicing their carrier landings at the direction of student landing signal officers or "paddles." His images, though functional and technically proficient, were not the epic documents his later carrier work would be.

Still, the experience proved valuable for the budding young photojournalist, as later in 1943 he would head to war on a carrier himself. For now, Miller had to settle for making the rounds of the American heartland, heading out February 13 to document Women Accepted for Volunteer Service—WAVES—the first of whom were undergoing training in Iowa, Wisconsin, and Indiana to be enlisted aviation sailors, freeing up men from shore billets so they could return to sea.

Inside the Douglas aircraft plant at El Segundo, California, in August 1943, women riveters work on a wing panel of an SBD Dauntless dive-bomber.

Miller followed the young women through the various parts of their training, photographing them marching, in their barracks cleaning, in class undergoing instruction, and even captured many as they left training and were boarding trains to head to their ultimate duty stations.

The images were poignant, often catching the women in unguarded moments, and one sees in them the sensitivity of Miller's mature work. His ability to capture moments with a freshness and immediacy would mark his work throughout the rest of the war and into his civilian photo career.

Victor Jorgensen, the last of the original six photographers to join the unit, reported for duty in Washington in January 1943 after finishing basic officer training in Tucson, Arizona.

Though he had been earmarked for Steichen's unit, Navy officials tried to divert Jorgensen to intelligence photo training in Pensacola, but the old man was able to nip that effort in the bud quickly to ensure that Jorgensen's original orders would hold.

Construction of aircraft at the Glenn L. Martin plant at Baltimore, Maryland, in early 1943. Machine-gun turrets are completely assembled and operated before installed in the carcass of PBM.

Hearing Jorgensen had reported, Steichen immediately ordered him to Naval Air Station Jacksonville, Florida, where he and Kerlee were again photographing aviation training efforts.

That's when Jorgensen got his first taste of Steichen's work pace.

"He was sixty-three, at that point, but he had more energy than the rest of us put together," Jorgensen said in an interview years later.

"At the point I got there, why, poor old Kerlee had been run right down to the knees—the day after I got there he went into the hospital for a rest and I drew the token of chasing Steichen around.

"It was really quite a job, he ran me ragged. He had a fabulous energy. He could go eighteen hours a day at a dead flat out and he'd do it."

From Jacksonville, the trio, with a now-rested Kerlee, headed down to Miami to visit the school where officers were taught how to hunt submarines on the high seas, and then on to the Banana River Naval Air Station near Cocoa Beach—the present sight of Patrick Air Force Base, where the Navy was training crews to handle flying boats of all kinds.

Arriving back in Washington in March, Steichen again walked into a hornet's nest of Navy bureaucracy as his age again came back to haunt him.

On March 27, 1943, his sixty-fourth birthday, he was informed that he had reached mandatory retirement age and was to be taken off the active duty list and would have to go home. Not one to give up easily, Steichen appealed to then Undersecretary of the Navy James Forrestal, who was able to keep the old man on active duty by using a relatively new federal statute allowing the Navy to bring back retired officers for service in special circumstances.

"Because of his exceptional youth, physical stamina, mental attitude and outstanding performance of duty it is recommended he be placed on the Honorary Retired List of the U.S. Naval Reserve and be ordered to continue on active duty," Forrestal wrote, in his effort to justify Steichen's continued active duty—a request that was quickly approved.

By this time, Captain Radford had been promoted to rear admiral and was on his way to the Pacific to command Carrier Division 11. Rear Admiral John S. McCain Sr., now head of the Bureau of Aeronautics, inherited Steichen and his unit in late 1942, and quickly grew to appreciate them as much as Radford did.

McCain was pleased with the coverage naval aviation was getting in the media and knew much of the credit went to Steichen and his unit. As a result, he wanted more, and felt a temporary promotion to full commander was in order, directing that a recommendation to this effect be made to the Navy's chief of personnel on Steichen's behalf, as promotions for those on the retired list were considered "out of line" and needed special consideration.

"The development of the Visual Unit of the Bureau of Aeronautics Training literature section, under his present supervision has been such that it is now highly desirable that the subject officer be promoted to higher rank," Captain R. F. Hickey, then aide to McCain, wrote in a letter of June 15, 1943.

Hickey noted, "The work of this group has resulted in a view among editors that naval photography is outstanding in its quality and coverage. The photographs of Steichen are eagerly sought after for reproduction.

"This has been of the greatest public relations value and has assisted greatly in keeping the Navy before the public, thus enhancing its already favorable reputation. In addition his work has been of tremendous importance in the procurement of aviation cadets."

Steichen's promotion was effective that month. He would stay with McCain even when the latter was promoted to vice admiral and given the job of deputy chief of naval operations (air).

At that point, Steichen's unit was moved up a rung on the administrative ladder and now came under the jurisdiction of the office of the chief of naval operations. This change officially began the unit's shift from covering aviation operations and training activities to nearly exclusive coverage of the Navy as a whole in combat zones.

Much of the unit's work was sent out by the Navy's public-relations office in Washington, D.C.

But there's no doubt that Steichen's close relationship with editors throughout the publishing industry also facilitated a more direct release route, as he is known to have directly marketed stories by himself and his offi-

cers that ended up being prominently displayed in *Life, Look,* the *New York Times Magazine, Popular Photography, Vogue, Art News Annual,* and, of course, *U.S. Camera.*

The Navy's own internal publications such as *All Hands* magazine and *Naval Aviation News,* also routinely used the unit's work, all without any credit.

By the end of the war, Navy offices in D.C. and at many bases were hanging photographs by Steichen's photographers next to paintings of historic battles and people from the Navy's past. Some are still hanging in Navy offices today.

Steichen himself had a number of them hanging in his office, including a backlit shot by Bristol of sailors doing calisthenics on the flight deck of the *Suwannee* while heading to the North African invasion.

It was also on board the *Suwannee* that Kerlee had gotten to know Captain Joseph J. "Jocko" Clark, who early in 1943 was called home to take command of the new aircraft carrier *Yorktown,* currently being built on the Elizabeth River in Portsmouth, Virginia, at the Norfolk Navy Yard.

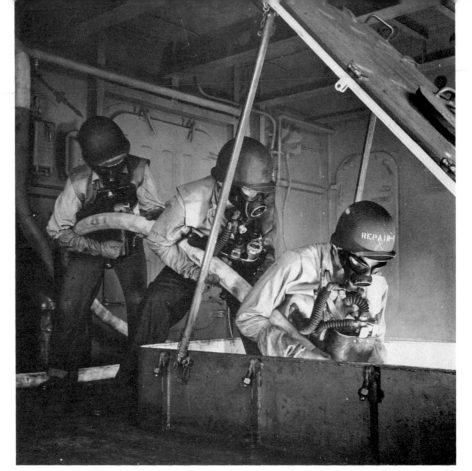

Damage-control teams conduct a firefighting drill at sea aboard the aircraft carrier Yorktown *during training prior to the ship deploying to the South Pacific in May 1943. The ship, commissioned in April 1943, was in combat by the fall.*

Kerlee arrived early and, along with motion-picture photographer Lieutenant Dwight Long, photographed the finishing touches being put on the ship and the final preparations being made for her commissioning.

The ship had been laid down four days before Pearl Harbor was attacked as the *Bon Homme Richard,* in honor of John Paul Jones's famous Revolutionary War ship. The name was changed to *Yorktown* to honor the previous ship of that name, sunk June 7, 1942, during the Battle of Midway.

The ship's sponsor was Eleanor Roosevelt, the nation's first lady, who seven years earlier had commissioned the first carrier to be named *Yorktown,* and Kerlee was on hand to document the proceedings, which almost ended in disaster.

With cameras running, the guest speaker was still in the middle of his speech when the ship started to slide down the ways to the river. Knowing that a warship hitting the water without a proper christening is destined to

Doubling as a transport, the flight deck of the carrier Yorktown *is lined end to end with jeeps, bound for action in the South Pacific as it is about to move under the Golden Gate Bridge. The vehicles were loaded on* Yorktown *during stopover in San Francisco heading to Pearl Harbor.*

have bad luck, Eleanor sprang to her feet, grabbed the bottle of champagne, and managed to break it across the bow just before it slipped out of her range.

As the word of her exploits spread through the crew and to other sailors, the first lady became quite popular with sailors. Particularly *Yorktown* sailors, who loved to retell the tale of her quick thinking.

Clark gave Kerlee an open-ended invitation to cover the ship's early days and spin-up for combat in the Pacific, based on his earlier association with Kerlee and Bristol's work on the *Suwannee* and *Santee*.

Kerlee took along with him Second-Class Specialist (Photography) Alfonso Iannelli, the Chicago commercial photographer who had been recruited by Steichen. Iannelli had ended up joining the Navy as an enlisted sailor because he lacked the national-level media credentials the others had before the war, but he was no less adept a photographer.

After the war, according to fellow Steichen unit enlisted man and camera repairman Marty Forscher, "Fons" Iannelli eventually became the highest paid of them all, working for *Fortune* magazine and even directing movies.

Unlike the strict caste system that existed in the fleet, there was more camaraderie between officers and enlisted men in the Steichen unit, and they tended to view one another more as peers, though the Navy forced them to eat and sleep apart when on board ship.

The only problems this created was that much of Iannelli's work was and still is credited to Kerlee. This included a famous picture, eventually selected by Steichen as one of the hundred best of the war, of *Yorktown* crewmen relaxing in their berthing areas, reading and writing letters.

But for now it was off to war, and the two photographers left Norfolk on May 21 as *Yorktown* completed her shakedown training in the vicinity of Trinidad in the Caribbean before returning to Norfolk on June 17 for a final tune-up and to take on supplies.

On July 1, 1943, the ship left Norfolk bound for the Pacific, first conducted flight operations in the Chesapeake Bay in order to get the crew used to her new air wing. On July 6, she headed for the Pacific via the Panama Canal.

During the July 11 and 12 transit of the Panama Canal, Kerlee disembarked by small boat and photographed the ship from front and rear in the canal's locks and inland waterways. He followed the ship's course on land to capture the transit.

Once she had cleared Balboa, the *Yorktown* headed straight to Pearl Harbor, where the crew would train for the war zone for the next month.

Arriving in Pearl Harbor on July 24, the ship began a month of workup exercises in the Hawaiian Islands. Finally, on August 22, she left Pearl and headed to war, with both Kerlee and Iannelli and motion-picture photographer Lieutenant Dwight Long on board.

It would be a quick hit for *Yorktown*'s first combat cruise. Iannelli documented the launches from on deck while Kerlee flew with the fighter escorts when the ship reached a launching point about 128 miles from Marcus Island early on August 31.

But it was a short-lived attack, lasting only one day, after which the *Yorktown* headed back to Pearl Harbor, arriving September 7 for a two-day stay before heading back to the United States to pick up aircraft and supplies.

Six days later, Kerlee, on board *Yorktown,* arrived in San Francisco and the crew spent the next two days feverishly loading aircraft, jeeps, trucks, stores, and just about any kind of supplies that would fit on her flight deck, hangar deck, and in her holds.

As Kerlee and Iannelli photographed, the *Yorktown* was transformed from fighting carrier to floating supply barge. Kerlee not only photographed the material being loaded onto the ship, but he made a famous image of the *Yorktown,* with row upon row of jeeps lined up on her flight deck, passing under the Golden Gate Bridge on September 15 as the ship departed again for Pearl.

By the twenty-ninth, the ship was again outfitted for war and left Hawaii on her second combat excursion into the South Pacific. By October 5, she was within striking distance of Wake Island, known in the United States at the time as the "Alamo of the Pacific."

The island had been the scene of an epic battle on December 11, 1941, when the Japanese, flush from their raid on Pearl Harbor and their invasion of the Philippines, decided to take the American possessions of Wake and Guam.

The United States had gradually been fortifying the island, which was considered of strategic importance in the Pacific as a fueling station and had been a stop on the Pan American Clipper flying boat's trans-Pacific route during the 1930s.

When the Japanese invaded, there were nearly three hundred Marines and over a thousand civilians on the island who managed to fight as a group and repulse the invaders on their first attempt, sinking three ships and killing over seven hundred Japanese in the process.

Their success had been so great that the United States was trying to rush more men and aircraft to reinforce the island, when on December 23, the Japanese returned. The Americans were only a day away when the second attempt to take the island occurred.

Afraid of losing the aircraft carrier *Saratoga* along with ships full of Marines to a larger Japanese force, American commanders had decided to turn back, stranding the remaining Marines and civilians, who surrendered to the Japanese.

In the nearly two years since that time, all of the Marines and most of the civilians had been evacuated from the island by the Japanese and sent to prison camps in China and Japan. But ninety-six of the civilians still remained.

Early on the morning of October 5, 1943, Kerlee boarded an SBD Dauntless dive-bomber on the *Yorktown*'s deck and flew off to photograph the island from the rear gunner's seat.

For two days, the *Yorktown*'s bombers pounded the island, now isolated by the U.S. advance in the Pacific and cut off from regular resupply from Japan. During the raids, the *Yorktown* and her sister

Aircraft fly close to the ocean with the aircraft carrier Yorktown *in the background. This photo was much published during the war and was also the cover image of Lieutenant Max Miller's book* Daybreak for our Carrier.

ship *Lexington* flew 510 sorties against the island, dropping 340 tons of bombs. Meanwhile, the accompanying destroyers and cruisers rained in nearly 3,200 rounds of five- and eight-inch shells.

Kerlee produced many outstanding photographs during those two days, including a famous shot of a fighter aircraft high above the *Yorktown* making a steep dive to get into position to land back on the carrier.

But his most famous photo, one that was published many times during the war and continued to be published after the war, is that of a silhouetted pilot in the open cockpit of his Dauntless dive-bomber several thousand feet above Wake Island, which is seen below the pilot and his aircraft. Smoke is rising from the bomb damage on the island.

Kerlee and his fellow sailors had no way of knowing if there were still Americans on the island. During the raids, the surviving American civilian prisoners were all in shelters and none were injured.

Unfortunately, the raids had a tragic result. On the day after the raid, Rear Admiral Shigematsu Sakaibara, the Japanese commander of the island, used the *Lexington* and *Yorktown* bombing raid as an excuse to commit an atrocity that would eventually cost him his life at the end of the war.

He ordered the commander of his headquarters company, Lieutenant Torashi Ito, to take the prisoners and execute them on a beach located on the northwestern most part of the island. The prisoners were then seated in a single line, facing out to sea, as Ito positioned his men behind them with rifles and machine guns.

When Ito gave the order, his men fired till all the prisoners were dead.

U.S. forces would continue to pound the island for the remainder of the war, but U.S. troops did not retake it until after the Japanese surrendered in August of 1945.

Working with Kerlee on this cruise was Lieutenant Carlton "Max" Miller. Miller had spent nearly twenty years as a reporter for the *San Diego Sun*; his "beat" had been covering the Navy and merchant marine as well as dockworkers.

Miller became famous when he wrote an autobiographical collection of

For sailors, church is wherever you can set up the altar. Here, divine services are being held in the hangar deck of the Yorktown *during operations in the South Pacific in the summer of 1943.*

Men read and relax aboard USS Yorktown *(CVA-10) in equatorial waters, October 1943.*

first-person stories about his time as a reporter. *I Cover The Waterfront* became a best seller and was made into a movie in 1936, setting Miller up for life.

No stranger to the Navy himself, he had served as an enlisted sailor in World War I. As a third-class quartermaster, Miller helped navigate transports across the Atlantic as part of convoys. After the war, he went to college in Washington State before starting his newspaper career in Everett, Washington, then moving on to San Diego.

In 1943, Miller was back in uniform, this time as an officer. His duty was to write books for the Navy.

Miller joined Kerlee on board the *Yorktown* as the pair collaborated on a book that described what life was like on board a Navy flattop; officials believed the book would explain to the American public the lot of the thousands of sailors serving on America's carriers and show how such ships operated.

The book, which would be called *Daybreak for Our Carrier,* was published in

March of 1944. Although it was created on board the *Yorktown,* the ship's name was never mentioned for fear of violating security.

"Not before now, to our knowledge, has there been so true and detailed a record of the day-to-day living and human reactions of a considerable body of men in the whole course of one operation against the enemy," reads the publisher's foreword. "Nor, more important, a record which is the work of officers who gathered their material on regular duty, not merely as correspondents or assigned observers. It is this fact, we believe, which gives such special quality to both Lieutenant Miller's text and Lieutenant Kerlee's photographs."

Rear Admiral Arthur C. Davis wrote the book's introduction, praising the authors for making carrier life easily understandable for the average American.

Seaman Second Class Lawrence Britton on duty at port lookout aboard USS Nassau *in October 1943. Lieutenant Wayne Miller rode the* Nassau *to the South Pacific in order to catch a ride on the aircraft carrier* Saratoga.

Davis was qualified to make this statement. He had been awarded the Navy Cross while the commanding officer of the carrier *Enterprise* during the Battle of the Eastern Solomon Islands. It was an epic sea battle in which, on August 24, 1942, the U.S. Navy finally stopped the "Tokyo Express" that had been seeking to reinforce the Japanese on Guadalcanal.

"The reader knows that Max Miller was there," Davis wrote. "Max writes about the things that matter the most when all is over. The reader, when he finishes, will have been there too and those who actually were along will live through it again—nothing yet written about naval aviation approaches the complete, satisfying lucidity—the clarity of daybreak in short—with which he sees and tells each incident."

It is also interesting to note that though the book was published by the Whittlesey House of the McGraw-Hill Book Company, the company, as was the case with many similar wartime projects, did not profit from its sales. All the content was produced by active-duty military and therefore in the public domain.

The proceeds instead were put into a fund that helped provide morale building and recreation for soldiers, sailors, airmen, and Marines serving worldwide.

Meanwhile, back in United States, Fenno Jacobs, who was a master at industrial photography, had been documenting the mobilization at home by traveling around the country to various aircraft manufacturing plants photographing the workers and planes they were producing.

His first stop was the Martin aircraft plant northeast of Baltimore, where he photographed large Martin Mariner flying boats being assembled.

Steichen so loved the results that he sent both Jacobs and Jorgensen to Arizona and California to visit four more aircraft plants.

The pair not only caught images of America's industrial might, they also created an excellent portrait of the people who worked in the plants. Their images had a documentary style to them that was reminiscent of Roy Stryker's Farm Security Administration work of the 1930s.

Though the images of the aircraft being assembled inside the factory are monuments to American industrial power, it's the images of the people that have probably been used the most in exhibits and textbooks over the past sixty years.

August 1943 was a busy month for the unit and one of great transition— for now the unit began to break away from its strict aviation training mandate and branch out into combat operations and explorations of other parts of the Navy as well.

In July and August, Jacobs, Jorgensen, and Steichen descended on the Navy's submarine base at Groton, Connecticut, and the electric-boat plant

Pharmacist's Mate Third Class John W. Galbreath waits on the Saratoga's flight deck for aircraft to return from raids on the Japanese stronghold of Rabaul on November 5, 1943.

located across the river in New London, then mass-producing submarines for the American war effort.

Their images, too, had that documentary feel and told the stories of the civilian workers and sailors who built and operated the vessels of the silent service.

These images were the unit's first real foray outside the original aviation mandate, but their results were no less spectacular. Here Jacobs again proved

his ability to produce outstanding industrial photos that often had a very human feel to them—for example, his image of a man holding a wrench, working on the pressure hull of a submarine, with a nearly completed submarine in the background, ready to be launched into the Thames River.

As the trio photographed submarines being built and outfitted, they often went along on short trips to sea, documenting crews training up and preparing to deploy. Some of the crews they photographed went on to have heroic patrols in the Pacific, while others came to tragic ends.

Some of Steichen's best images from this trip are of a commanding officer inspecting his sailors, decked out in their dress-white uniforms on the narrow foredeck of a submarine.

He and the others also made a number of images inside submarines showing crews at work. Jacobs's best work of the trip was done in a documentary "slice of life" style, catching one sailor eating a sandwich while sitting under the tail end of a torpedo—another view shows two sailors in their bunks on board a submarine joking while two massive torpedoes sit underneath their bunks.

Jacobs captured Ship's Cook Second Class Peter Grabnickas in his bunk on board the submarine *Capelin,* reading the book *The Stray Lamb* by Thorne Smith, surrounded by at least seven "girlie" pictures.

The picture takes on a haunting dimension since Grabnickas, a native of Malverne, New York, would die just five months later when the *Capelin* and her crew of seventy-eight were lost on December 1, 1943, when the sub was caught on the surface by Japanese patrol aircraft while returning to Australia after her second war patrol. She went down with all hands.

A few of these images made it into the October 1943 issue of the Navy's *All Hands* magazine, where they came to the attention of Rear Admiral Freeland A. Daubin, the Atlantic Fleet's submarine commander.

The article highlighted the life of submarine sailors in an attempt to get

OPPOSITE: *With sailors packing every available observation perch, the aircraft carrier* Yorktown *moves through the Panama Canal for the first time in her career, heading to the Pacific through the Culebra Cut in July 1943.*

more volunteers for duty in the silent service. One of Jacobs's images of sailors on lookout in a submarine conning tower took the cover of the magazine, while Steichen's dress-white inspection photo was spread across two pages along with the magazine's contents.

Daubin wrote to McCain at the Bureau of Aeronautics on October 30, 1943, commending Steichen and Jacobs by name, calling their photographs "remarkable."

"It is considered that these pictures have considerable value for training purposes and that they will serve as an incentive towards getting more suitable volunteers for submarine duty," Daubin wrote. "It is requested that the appreciation of Commander, Submarines Atlantic Fleet, be extended to Commander Steichen and Lt. Jacobs for the excellence of their work, for the interest which they took in this project and for the assistance which they have rendered the submarine service."

Horace Bristol would soon find out that it wasn't just Navy carriers that were fighting an air war. His second trip into combat took him to the Aleutian Islands off Alaska, where the Japanese had invaded U.S. territory.

Though Midway had ended in disaster for them, the Japanese managed to take and hold both Attu and Kiska islands. The United States wanted those islands back, and the battle for Attu was in full swing when Bristol arrived May 28, just days before the Allies managed to secure Attu, effectively cutting off Kiska from Japan and any hopes of regular resupply.

For the next two months, the United States waged an aerial campaign against Kiska and Bristol played an important part.

He documented the aircraft and men of the Navy's patrol air wings operating flying boats out of Seattle, creating some of his most outstanding color images of the war. One particularly famous view shows a U.S. Navy patrol of flying boats passing snow-covered peaks on the mountainous islands. Also, his black-and-white images of sailors on and off the job in remote Alaska are technical marvels and show a little-seen part of the Navy.

His images of a forward air base during a blizzard show how tough life could be for these sailors who served in flying boats instead of ships.

An F6F aircraft descends the deck elevator to the hangar deck while other aircraft await their turn and still others circle, awaiting the chance to land after returning from raids on the Japanese stronghold of Rabaul on November 5, 1943 .

Bristol's photography was also used to plan targets during the nearly two-month bombardment of Kiska as well as in the planning of the invasion that happened on August 15.

"Mr. Bristol is a photographer of superior technical ability and artistic talent," wrote then Captain Leslie Gehres, commander of Fleet Air Wing 4, in a confidential letter intended for inclusion in Bristol's semiannual fitness report. "During this period, he was assigned as photographer of a combat crew engaged in photographing, under fire of anti-aircraft batteries, enemy positions and beaches on Kiska Island."

Lieutenant Harold Robinson, landing signal officer, on board the aircraft carrier Saratoga, gives the pilot the signal to cut power just before landing on deck.

Those photographs were "of great assistance in planning the landing of our forces," Gehres went on to write, explaining that Bristol not only took many of the photos himself, he also trained the wing's other enlisted photo personnel in using and processing color film.

From his time in combat over North Africa, Bristol had qualified to wear the Navy's coveted "combat aircrew" wings, second in stature only to the gold Navy pilot's wings. His time over Kiska would qualify him to add a gold star, signifying he'd been in even more aerial combat.

But the invasion was anticlimactic in the end. When the U.S. forces landed on August 15, they found an empty island—over the weeks of bombardment, the Japanese managed to use submarines to gradually sneak all their soldiers off the island.

Meanwhile, now Lieutenant Junior Grade Wayne Miller had managed to get his first assignment outside the United States, accompanying a naval mission on a three-month-long trip to Brazil in search of quartz for use in military radios.

While on this trip, he spent time documenting the Naval Air Transport Service, known in the service as NATS, which was flying the contingent around. NATS was a combination Navy airline and air cargo transport service.

His images of these sailors who ferried men and gear around the world are among the only record of this part of the naval service during the war.

The leadership of the transport service liked Miller's images so much that they invited him along on other cross-country jogs in their aircraft, which took him from Seattle to the Caribbean Islands.

Background: *A South Carolina class battleship screens the carrier* Lexington's *starboard side during operations in the South Pacific in November 1943.*

The unit was coming of age, quickly, keeping pace with the war. Christopher Phillips, author of the 1980 book *Steichen at War*, a compilation of many of the unit's iconic works, wrote that it was around this time that the photographers began to refer to themselves as "Steichen's chickens" because of the way they scattered in all directions and seldom saw one another.

Jorgensen would later write that the term also indicated just how much "the old man brooded over us like a mother hen."

Steichen, too, would get out into the war zone, traveling first with Victor Jorgensen to Pearl Harbor and then, with Radford's help, to sea on an aircraft carrier.

Aircraft handlers "respot" or move an aircraft to another location on the flight deck of the Saratoga *to make room for other aircraft to land.*

On October 31, with Jorgensen in tow, he left San Francisco on the Pan Am Clipper with nearly six hundred pounds of cameras, film, and lighting equipment, bound for Pearl Harbor.

Not long after their arrival, word got around Hawaii that the famous Steichen was in town to take pictures and it seemed like a line started forming immediately among the brass to have their pictures taken.

"There was a riot before we went on the *Lexington*," recalled Jorgensen. "We hit Pearl Harbor and all the admirals wanted a Steichen photograph . . ." So, the old man agreed to do it, and so we set up shop out there on Ford Island, and had a parade of a whole works of them come by . . . we worked on that

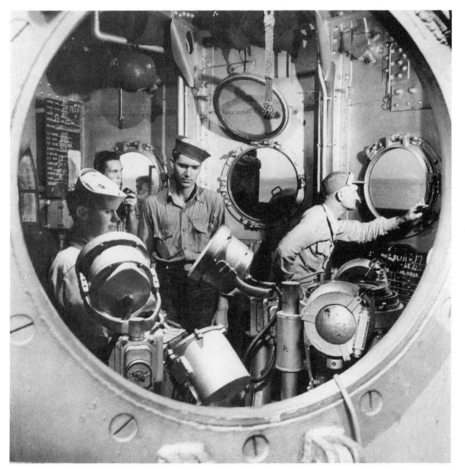

A unique view of the Saratoga's navigational bridge was shot by Lieutenant Wayne Miller through a portal. Here he captured watchstanders and the Saratoga's captain, John H. Cassidy, operating the ship in the South Pacific.

Pilots from Fighter Squadron 16 lean on the wing of an F6F Hellcat fighter after having one of the most extraordinary flying days of the war—seventeen confirmed kills and four probable from a flight of twenty-one enemy aircraft on November 23, 1943. Fourth from the right is Ensign Ralph Hanks, of Philadelphia, Pennsylvania, who became the first U.S. pilot to score being an "ace in a day," knocking out five of the enemy aircraft himself.

thing about two weeks before we got through them all. But I think we shot every darn one of them."

Portrait sessions done, Steichen and Jorgensen moved aboard the brand new aircraft carrier *Lexington* on November 9, as the ship prepared for sea.

Tied up near the *Lex* was her younger sister ship, the *Yorktown*.

Kerlee and Iannelli had left the ship and headed back to Washington, though motion-picture cameraman Lieutenant Dwight Long remained on board and Steichen spent several hours visiting with him and even made a call on Captain John "Jocko" Clark, who had become a great fan of Steichen's unit and their work and was praised by Steichen in 1947 for "the great way he backed our photographic projects."

On board the *Lexington,* Steichen enjoyed certain privileges that personal fame, more than his Navy rank, entitled him to, including the best accommodations on the ship.

The captain of a ship the size of an aircraft carrier has two bunks. While at sea, he stays in what Steichen described in *The Blue Ghost,* his account of his *Lexington* adventures, as a "tiny cubical, his sea cabin, up on the bridge."

As the ship's commanding officer, Captain Felix Stump would be living and working high in the ship's island; he offered Steichen the use of his "in-port cabin," the more ornate and ceremonial set of rooms where the captain lives and entertains while in port.

This, Steichen wrote, "means not only personal comfort, but space for laying out our camera equipment . . . Vic and I spent a good part of the night discussing our plans."

Steichen was granted free run of the *Lexington,* and Stump apparently liked to use the ship's public-address system—the same one that "calls away" reveille, general quarters, and taps—to advise the photographer, and the whole crew, of interesting goings-on that could make interesting photos.

Steichen did not shy away from the hazardous situations on deck during takeoff and landing operations. It was on the second day at sea, when he was shooting pictures of the ship's landing signal officer at work, that an off-course aircraft nearly ran him over.

The LSOs, as they were called, tackled Steichen and the group fell into the safety net, which kept them from plunging into the Pacific Ocean.

But for all his own daring, Steichen was reluctant to let Jorgensen join the ship's pilots and aircrew when they flew into battle.

"I didn't hire you to get you killed," he insisted. Jorgensen, nonetheless, found his way aloft and took many aerial photos of the ship and their aircraft.

Eventually, he was awarded the coveted combat aircrew wings for his efforts, which by war's end held two battle stars, signifying that he had taken part in at least three separate battles and actually come under enemy fire.

While on the ship, the two men worked together sometimes, but more often worked apart, capturing all aspects of life on the carrier, with a particular emphasis on the flight-deck personnel and the pilots and aircraft. Not only did they capture the battle scenes, they also accurately portrayed the way sailors while away the long periods of waiting for combat by playing cards, jacks, and mumblety-peg or simply sleeping on the deck.

Musician First Class Glen Stankwitz catches up on his reading during a down period aboard the aircraft carrier Saratoga in the South Pacific.

In his book about Steichen, Phillips wrote that some of the pair's interior scenes might have been staged. This is almost certainly the case for some images, such as the ones shot in the ship's combat information center, of which there are several different views of what seems to be the same situation in the National Archives collection.

Such staging, however, was necessary, as Steichen often had to set up chains of one or more flashbulbs to brighten a situation in the low light of a ship's interior spaces. Those bulbs would have to be changed between exposures—making it difficult to simply capture events as they happened.

In the end, the photos seem to be a mix of set-up and unplanned moments—but no more so than what happens even to this day. The staged feel of the CIC is balanced by the documentary feel of many of the tense images portrayed in squadron ready rooms—such as that of a young pilot nervously yawning as he awaits the word to "man your planes."

Steichen made the most of his photographic knowledge and desire to experiment in capturing the "real" situations as well. For example, he used slow shutter speeds in multiple frames of an aircraft preparing for flight and launching from in front of the island.

"In all the take-off pictures I had seen, the planes looked as though they were glued to the deck," Steichen wrote in his autobiography. "I was going to try to give a sense of motion of the rushing plane. Instead of making a fast exposure to stop the motion and get a sharp picture of the plane taking off, I made a series of exposures at a 10th of a second."

The result was an image in which the ship's island—the background—is tack sharp, but the aircraft on deck is a blur of motion.

In another shot of the same island, he used infrared film for dramatic effect—making the ship and sky eerily dark while all the humans moving around on the island and flight deck appear normally lighted—providing not only visual contrast but a dramatic punch.

The only thing Steichen regretted was that there was no way to capture the deafening symphony of sound that also accompanies flight-deck operations.

Steichen felt the dramatic switch from boredom to terror a couple of times on the trip, but none as dramatic as the one that took place on December 4, 1943, during strikes on Kwajalein, 2,100 nautical miles southwest of Honolulu.

Steichen was on deck all day. The ship's morning strike destroyed a cargo ship, damaged two cruisers, and shot down thirty enemy aircraft.

Meanwhile, on deck, he witnessed the ship's antiaircraft gunners splash two of the enemy torpedo planes during a midday attack.

But the worst was yet to come. With the ship still at general quarters, Steichen photographed through the waning light—"making longer exposures, [I] hope there is still enough daylight to produce printable images on film."

At 7:20 pm, the gunners again opened up to fight off yet another enemy attack, but the Japanese persisted, and at nearly eleven-thirty, the enemy used parachute flares to illuminate the ship, silhouetting it against the dark night and making it an easier target to hit.

"With a sinking feeling comes the thought, now the covers are off . . . we are naked and we'll have to fight it out with the bastards," Steichen wrote in *The Blue Ghost*.

Ten minutes later, four Japanese aircraft were spotted and the ship's gunners opened up again.

"The tracer shells suddenly illuminate the underside of a Jap plane as it banks sharply to the right and gets away without being hit," he wrote. "That Jap was too close. I am holding my breath."

Suddenly, Steichen described, the ship "gave a thumping bounce, followed by violent up and down, whipping movements along the full length of the ship."

A torpedo had hit on the ship's starboard side, knocking out its steering and one of her massive propellers, putting the vessel into a permanent thirty-degree turn as the rudders were frozen in place.

Steichen began to think that the ship might sink if the damage became worse—and things were heading downhill, he thought, as the ship was five feet lower in the water aft than at the bow and dense clouds of smoke were pouring from ruptured fuel tanks.

It wasn't the first time such a scenario had crossed his mind. Earlier, during the boring transit to the war zone, Steichen and Jorgensen had discussed what they'd do if faced with having to swim for their lives.

"We discussed various means of keeping a camera dry in case we should have to abandon ship," he wrote. The two came up with the idea of using an aerographer's large rubber balloon (which sends aloft weather-forecasting gear) as a waterproof bag, and often practiced as a team to perfect the technique.

But during the actual battle, Jorgensen was nowhere in sight; he was off covering the action in other parts of the ship.

"It's a simple matter to get a camera in such a balloon when there are four hands," Steichen wrote. "I find myself using every possible combination of two

BACKGROUND: *The carrier* Enterprise *steams in the South Pacific during the Gilbert Island Campaign in November 1943.*

hands and my teeth . . . I hold the camera between my teeth and make futile attempts to force it into the narrow mouth of the rubber bag. This goes on for some time with a stupid sort of patience, but no success."

Steichen's ungraceful ballet caught the eye of Captain Stump.

"What are *you* trying to do?" Stump asked Steichen with a puzzled look on his face.

"I'm trying to get this dammed camera into a rubber bag so it will stay dry when we go over the side," Steichen replied.

"You won't need that," Stump replied with a chuckle as the entire bridge crew saw Steichen's clumsy efforts and broke into laughter. "You're not going over the side."

Steichen said that Stump headed over to the ship's PA system and told the entire crew what most already knew—that the ship had been hit by a torpedo—and assured them that all would be well if everyone did his job calmly and efficiently.

"Don't worry!" he said. "That's my job, I got you in here and I'll get you out."

A few hours later, the damage-control parties managed to straighten out the ship's rudders and the crew steered the ship by manually turning the rudders directly on top of them while varying the speed of the engines for the fine adjustments to the course.

By this time, the moon had set and Steichen decided to head to his stateroom to get some sleep. He'd had his baptism by fire and had survived.

In his quarters, he found the captain's Filipino stewards huddled together in the galley, fully attired in their battle dress of life jackets and helmets.

Steichen coaxed them out of their hiding place and told them what Stump had told the crew and that the attack was over, at least for now. Just then he opened the door that led to the office and his sleeping quarters and found Jorgensen fast asleep on the office couch.

"I motion to stewards to have a look, when they see the cherubic sleeping Vic they grin broadly, take off their tin hats and life preservers and head for their own quarters."

Three hours later, Steichen was up again and photographing the battle damage and weary sailors in their battle gear sleeping on the flight deck.

The night's toll had been two confirmed dead and seven missing in the flooded after spaces destroyed by the torpedo. In addition, thirty-five had been wounded.

The two confirmed were sailors killed instantly at their battle stations when the torpedo hit.

They would be buried at sea the next day. Steichen and Jorgensen documented the event as the Marine honor guard fired a salute, the sailors tilted the stretchers holding their fallen shipmates, and the bodies in their weighted bags slipped into the sea, while a bugler blew taps.

The missing men would be later pulled from the *Lex*'s mangled stern once the ship arrived back at Pearl.

Lieutenant Commander Paul D. Buie, commanding officer of Fighter Squadron 16 on board the aircraft carrier Lexington, *describes his squadron's nearly perfect day against Japanese carrier aircraft on November 23, 1943. Buie himself shot down two aircraft.*

"The faces of the men standing by reflect their thinking and wondering . . . it might have been you . . . it might have been me . . . next time it may be any one of us. Back home a mother will soon receive a telegram she will never forget. A message she will never quite adjust herself to," Steichen wrote in *The Blue Ghost*. Never again would he look at a full moon as he had done before the battle, he said in later life.

By this time, the *Lexington* was out of danger and heading back to Pearl Harbor, where it arrived on December 9 for temporary repairs. Steichen would stay on board until December 23, by which time the *Lexington* had made it all the way to the Navy's shipyard in Bremerton, Washington, for permanent repairs. Steichen left the ship with mixed emotions for a Christmas reunion with his wife, Dana.

The youngest member of the team, Lieutenant Wayne Miller, would have

Heavy seas cause a curtain of water to partially obscure a Navy tanker ship as it refuels the carrier Lexington *at sea during November 1943. Refueling at sea allows the U.S. Navy to steam for long distances at high speed—a fact that led to the Navy's success in World War II.*

the closest call during those early combat days aboard the carrier *Saratoga* in the South Pacific.

He'd gotten his first taste of carrier life on the high seas aboard the "jeep" carrier *Nassau* as it ferried aircraft to the South Pacific in late summer and early fall 1943.

That small carrier would be his ride to the war zone, but it would be aboard the aircraft carrier *Saratoga* that Miller's life changed forever.

The third carrier built by the United States, the *Sara,* was actually completed and commissioned one month before her sister ship, the *Lexington,* sank at the Battle of the Coral Sea in 1942. She would be the oldest carrier to make it through to the end of the war afloat.

By the time Miller joined the ship in Pearl Harbor on October 29, 1943, it had been damaged in battle by Japanese torpedoes in early September of 1942 and had returned to service.

The United States was planning to invade the island of Bougainville—the next stop in the island-hopping strategy—but close by was a Japanese naval base at Simpson Harbor on the island of Rabaul, where the Imperial Navy was massing ships to counter the U.S offensive.

Admiral Chester Nimitz sent the *Saratoga* and the smaller "jeep" carrier *Princeton* to cover the November 1 Marine landings on Bougainville by knocking out the Japanese air bases on the nearby islands of Buka and Bonis. As a result, the United States owned the skies over the island as the Marines fought their way ashore.

But intelligence reports showed the Japanese massing surface ships at Rabaul. Nimitz knew that if left alone, these ships could decimate the U.S. efforts off Bougainville, so the *Saratoga* and *Princeton* were sent to attack.

Heavy casualties were predicted by the U.S. high command, but there was no other choice.

"There was tension throughout the ship," Miller recalled. "Tension because we all knew that we were sailing into the mouth of the dragon."

On board the *Saratoga,* Air Wing 12 prepared for the attack. In the wing were three squadrons, one for bombing, one for torpedoes, and a fighter squadron to provide cover and do battle with Japanese aircraft.

The date was set for November 5, but with no time for detailed preparation, the decision was made by Commander Henry Caldwell, Group 12's commander, to direct the attack from the air in real time while over Rabaul.

Miller had made arrangements to be inside Caldwell's plane, giving him a front-row seat for the attack. On the evening of November 5, just hours before the attack was to take place, he was preparing his gear for the next day in his stateroom when a knock came at his door.

Opening up the door, Miller was surprised to see that his guest was an enlisted man, that is, someone who was not supposed to be in "officers' country" unless on official business. It was Photographer's Mate First Class Paul T. Barnett, an enlisted photographer assigned to the *Sara's* air group.

"Lieutenant Miller, I understand you've made arrangements to be in the commander's plane tomorrow—is that true?" Barnett asked.

When Miller confirmed that this was the plan, Barnett continued. He was

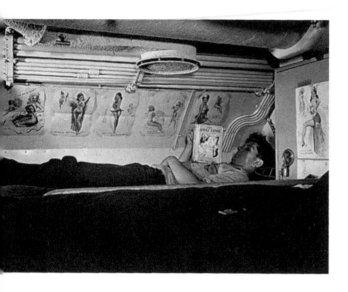

Ship's Cook Second Class Peter Grabnickas, of Melverne, New York, relaxes in his rack with a book on board the submarine Capelin *as the ship fitted out in New London in August 1943. On December 1, Grabnickas and the other seventy-five officers and men on board died when their sub disappeared seventeen days into her second war patrol in the South Pacific off Australia.*

nearing the end of his assignment on the *Saratoga* and had not yet flown into combat, and he desperately wanted the experience before transferring later in the month. "Well, I hope you won't pull rank on me, but I want to take your place tomorrow, I want to be in that plane," he told Miller.

"Sure, I had the rank and I could have told him no," Miller recalled. "I just couldn't do that, so I told him okay, the flight was his."

The next morning, Miller was on deck early as the pilots began to man their planes. He photographed all the major players of the day, including Caldwell and his fighter squadron commander, Lieutenant Commander "Jumping" Joe Clifton. He even photographed Barnett as he adjusted his gear and prepared to get inside Caldwell's TBF Avenger.

"I photographed all the squadron commanders as they got in their aircraft and I saw Barnett as he was preparing to get into the seat behind Caldwell," Miller recalled.

Now more of an observer than a participant, Miller turned his attention to photograph the flight-deck crews and the launch of the air wing toward Rabaul.

Once all the aircraft were gone, Miller photographed men sitting around loudspeakers, waiting for any word of how the battle was going over 150 miles away. He also made a portrait of a young Navy corpsman standing in his battle dress with his helmet blazoned with a red cross inside a white circle, his first-aid kit over his shoulder and uncertainty in his eyes.

Though updates were given over the ship's loudspeaker and everybody knew there'd be losses, particulars had to wait until all aircraft had been recovered.

"We'd heard they'd had a rough go of it," Miller said. "But we didn't know yet the extent of it."

High above Rabaul, Caldwell's Avenger was escorted by two Hellcat fighters as it circled the harbor.

The attack had gone well, so well in fact that it was called one of the war's most spectacular raids—and the *Saratoga*'s finest hour of the war.

Though no Japanese ships were sunk, six had been damaged and four of those heavily—that enemy task force was not going anywhere. Losses on the American side had been light. Just ten U.S. aircraft from the carriers had been downed, while American planes had downed or destroyed on the ground fifty enemy aircraft. The *Saratoga* itself never even saw enemy aircraft that day.

Barnett had been photographing the harbor below when suddenly the trio of planes were surprised by a group of Japanese Zero fighters. While the Hellcat escort went to work, Caldwell tried to keep his attention on directing the attack even though a Zero was heading straight toward the middle of his aircraft, machine guns blazing.

In the hail of bullets, Caldwell's aircraft became disabled and Barnett was killed instantly; the aircraft's other passenger, Aviation Ordnanceman Kenneth Bratton, was wounded. The last photograph in Barnett's camera was a single frame of the Zero—heading straight at Caldwell's Avenger.

As the aircraft began to return, the ship recovered the other aircraft and then prepared to bring Caldwell's shot-up bird aboard.

Only one of the aircraft's landing gear was functioning, the pilot had no use of his flaps, and his radio was out—so no one on board knew that Barnett—sitting in the exact spot Miller had been slated for—had died.

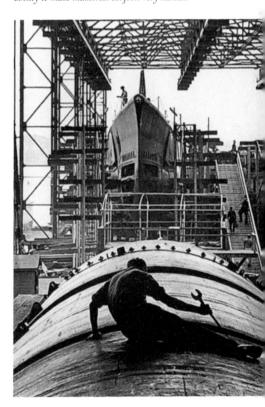

A civilian shipyard worker tightens bolts in the hull of a U.S. submarine being built at the Electric Boat Company in Groton, Connecticut, in this picture shot by Lieutenant Charles Fenno Jacobs, who had the ability to make industrial subjects very human.

"When the plane landed, there was a huge hole in the fuselage," Miller said. "When they flipped up the door under where the radioman sits, there was Barnett, dead, and he had been shot up quite badly."

Miller photographed litter crews removing Barnett's body from the shot-up aircraft.

Meanwhile, Miller went around to the other side of the ship, where flight-deck crews were working hard to extract Bratton, wounded in the legs from his gunner's seat in the aircraft's rear. Miller made a number of frames of a grimacing Bratton being pulled from the aircraft. One of these has become one of the war's iconic photographs.

But Miller didn't stop to think about it all and went on to photograph other wounded aircrew being attended to. Though there had been casualties, the overall mood was jubilant and Miller even photographed fighter-squadron commander Clifton handing out cigars and later participating in his other favorite pastime—eating ice cream.

But it would all catch up with Miller later, in the quiet of his stateroom.

"It affected me quite a bit as I felt very guilty about giving up my spot to Barnett and he caught it," Miller said. "At the same time I knew that is what he wanted . . . I was terribly confused by it, but that's the way it is . . . strange things like that happen in war . . ."

Later, Miller said he thought of that day often, but knew in his mind he had to press on, though pressing on started with shooting the burial at sea the next day, as well as taking photographs of the chief petty officer and a helper going through the personal belongings of the dead, preparing them for shipment to the next of kin.

Miller didn't only shoot combat. His work from the *Saratoga* is a complete document of life on the ship, from men playing cards and relaxing in their berthing areas to potatoes being peeled in the galley. Miller poked his head into almost every area of the ship with good results.

When some of the *Saratoga*'s air wing moved ashore to help cover the Marine landings on Tarawa, Miller again wanted to go, but there was no room in the one-seat fighter aircraft.

Adak Harbor in the Aleutians, with part of huge U.S. fleet at anchor, ready to move against Kiska. Bristol photographed this breathtaking view from his seat in a Navy PBY-5A patrol bomber in August 1943.

Instead, he agreed to have himself placed in an interior part of the aircraft. Literally bolted inside the aircraft, Miller would not be able to escape, even if the plane ditched at sea.

He survived the ordeal to document the aircraft during their temporary shore stay and repeated the process to return to the *Saratoga* when it was all done.

Miller left the *Saratoga* on December 6 and arrived back in Washington on December 11 to oversee the processing and captioning of his shipboard work. His photos received wide distribution and made Bratton a hero who would go on to conduct war-bond drives with Miller's picture of the wounded ord-nanceman in the background.

Miller returned to the *Saratoga* on December 23 as the ship underwent repairs in San Francisco and was on board on January 13, 1944, as the ship got under way again for the South Pacific. Miller shot the invasion of the island of Enigbi from the air, much as Bristol had done in North Africa.

The *Saratoga* was then dispatched via Australia for the Indian Ocean to support British naval operations there. Eventually Miller photographed British Admiral Lord Mountbatten on board the ship and even inspecting and speaking to the crew.

A Grumman F6F-3 Hellcat fighter from Fighter Squadron 5 makes condensation rings as it awaits the takeoff flag clearing it to launch from the aircraft carrier Yorktown *on November 20, 1943, for missions hitting targets in the Marshall Islands during landings.*

October 6, 1943: Lieutenant Commander Charles Kerlee spent four hours standing behind the pilot in an identical SBD Dauntless dive-bomber during raids on Wake Island from the aircraft carrier Yorktown. Japanese facilities can be seen burning below.

Pilots make reports to the squadron intelligence officer (far right) in the ready room after returning to the aircraft carrier Yorktown *from a mission in June 1944.*

Photographer's Mate First Class Paul T. Barnett adjusts his flight gear prior to getting into the TBF Avenger for the raids on Rabaul, November 5, 1943. A few hours later, Barnett was dead, killed by a Japanese Zero. Lieutenant Wayne Miller had reluctantly given up his seat on the aircraft, piloted by air group Commander Howard Caldwell.

Enlisted gunner Kenneth Bratton, an aviation ordnanceman, is lifted from the shattered cockpit of a TBF aircraft after the raid on Rabaul on November 5, 1943. Bratton would survive the war and the photo. The fame it brought him sent on a nationwide bond drive.

The hole in this aircraft was made by a 20mm shell from a Japanese Zero fighter that hit the aircraft during the November 5 raid on Rabaul. The gunner in the seat was killed immediately and when his body was removed, flight-deck crews had to pry his fingers off his .50-caliber machine gun to remove his body.

Commander "Jumping" Joe Clifton, commander of the Saratoga's fighter squadron, celebrates after his return from Rabaul by passing out cigars on the hangar deck of the ship.

Lieutenant Wayne Miller did this portrait of the Saratoga's *captain, John H. Cassidy, on the bridge of the ship while operating in the South Pacific.*

Officers and sailors work in the chart room, plotting the aircraft carrier Lexington *and her task group as the ship moves into position for strikes on the Marshall and Gilbert Islands in December 1943 .*

A PBY-5A Catalina Patrol bomber flies over the snow-covered Aleutian Islands during the retaking of the Alaskan Islands during the spring and summer of 1943.

Captain Edward Steichen examines the photographic work of Specialist First Class (P) Fred Fleischman in early 1945. Steichen reviewed the work of many sailors seeking to enter his elite photo unit.

New Arrivals

☆   ☆   ☆

IN THE YEARS following the war, many who served in Navy photography were fond of saying, "I served with Steichen." As with many elite units, if everyone who claimed membership in the Aviation Photographic Unit actually served in it, its membership would have been in the hundreds.

But for many of those claimants, their boasts could be partially true. Steichen was always on the lookout for talent. His primary search was for officer photographers for his special unit, but when he found a talented, motivated shooter, whatever his rank, he worked to place him in one of the Navy's combat photo units.Steichen did this throughout the war, but in mid-1945, he formally took control of all Navy Combat Photography, which by that time was working primarily in the Pacific theater—though his responsibility included any Navy combat photo unit worldwide. The photo units were small and mobile, consisting of a photographic officer, two motion-picture cameramen, and one still photographer.

Officer photographers in these combat units sometimes doubled as the head of the team while at the same time going off on assignments to take pictures themselves. Many images from these photographers are credited to the Steichen unit even though the shooters might not have been connected to it formally.

Steichen was a tough boss. The old man pulled no punches and many a photographer was sent away in defeat if not tears after Steichen reviewed his portfolio of images.

Others had better luck. Marion Warren, a Navy first-class photographer's mate, was a good example. His meeting with Steichen was successful because the aging photographer saw promise in the young man. A beginning photographer before the war, Warren had joined the Navy with a dream to become a combat photographer. Instead, he ended up in Washington, D.C., in and out of the offices of the brass, photographing people getting medals or shooting portraits. He even spent a week with famed Canadian portrait photographer Yosef Karsh, who came to D.C. to shoot his own portraits of the U.S. Navy's leadership.

It would be in mid-1945 when Warren would get a break.

"One of the friends of mine in the public relations office, I found out, was a very good friend of Edward Steichen," Warren recounted to his daughter Mame years after the war.

Application photo of Barrett Gallagher is from official Navy service jacket.

"I got my friend to get me an appointment with Steichen. The admiral sent down word that he wanted me to bring a lot of pictures—not fancy, dressy pictures, but contact prints or eight by tens; he didn't care. Of course, I was scared stiff."

As a sailor, he was afraid of meeting a Navy captain, and professionally, Warren knew he was about to face the top commercial photographer of the time—both daunting prospects.

"He took my stack of fifty or more pictures and went through them like dealing a deck of cards. I resented that because I couldn't look at pictures that fast and I didn't think he could. Finally, he came to a picture of a couple dancing. It only showed them from the waist down with rolled socks on the gal and suede shoes on the man and their hands. He looked at that picture for a minute or two and he looked back at me and he said, 'Young man, you make pictures like this and you can be a good photographer someday.'"

Warren remembered Steichen shuffling through more images and noticed him stop to look awhile at one. Feeling brave, he quickly said, "Sir, that was only made with a small folding camera."

What Steichen said in reply stayed with Warren throughout his career: "Young man, there's not a photographer alive can make full use of a box camera. For the rest of his career, Warren would recall those words whenever he was contemplating buying a "fancy piece of equipment" or other photo gear he thought he couldn't do without.

Warren claims that single comment from Steichen saved him a lot of money over the years.

"I'd [ask myself], 'Do I really need that to do this job?' Usually I didn't," Warren said. So, with that mental debate in mind, he'd ponder the purchase a few more days and usually decide against it.

In the end, the good news was that Steichen accepted Warren into Combat Photography. The bad news was that the war ended before he could get his orders to go to the Pacific.

Among the most active of the new photographers who were added to the Steichen unit was Barrett Gallagher, who turned out to be not only an excellent photographer but also a highly decorated sailor as well, being awarded medals for valor and not photography.

It's a miracle that Gallagher didn't end up as an artillery officer in the Army, slogging his way across Europe during World War II with a large cannon instead of a small, handheld camera. But even more of a miracle was how, as a young gunnery officer in the Atlantic, he survived two years of convoy duty before entering Steichen's unit.

A young man and a 1936 graduate of Cornell University, Gallagher had run his own photo studio in New York City before the war. He didn't look much like a naval officer. His boyish looks and round face seemed more appropriate in a high school debate team than on the deck of a ship. But looks can be deceiving.

His interest in things military began years before, when he was a boy in Virginia. For three years he attended the now defunct Staunton Military Academy, an institution that for 116 years was a military high school, sending many boys on to places like West Point and the Virginia Military Academy.

Gallagher almost ended up at West Point himself, winning an automatic appointment as the school's top student in military science at the end of his

Lieutenant Barrett Gallagher sits in the rear seat of a Curtis SB2C Helldiver dive-bomber that has just landed on the deck of the aircraft carrier Lexington *in the South Pacific. Gallagher was attached to the staff of Rear Admiral Gerald Bogan on the* Lexington *at the time.*

third year—an unheard-of feat, as the award normally only went to someone in his fourth year and usually to one with some rank in the cadet hierarchy.

"It was quite unheard of for a third year to beat out fourth year cadets," Gallagher said in later years. "Amazingly I was even able to beat out the Cadet Major—the top cadet in the school—who at the time was the future Senator and future presidential candidate Barry Goldwater."

But Gallagher bypassed West Point to attend Cornell University in Ithaca, New York. It was the family school and he wanted to follow in the footsteps of his mother and father and sister.

Japanese soldiers climb out of rocks and bushes on small island of Kerama-retto off Okinawa, Japan, and into water to give themselves up to crew of picket boat, in May 1945.

That doesn't mean he gave up on the military, though. Instead, he took four years of Army Reserve Officer Training Corps. At the time, Cornell's ROTC unit specialized in teaching artillery, a skill that, in Gallagher's case, would prove invaluable later to the Navy and not the Army.

He graduated in 1936 with a bachelor of arts degree in public speaking. But he missed the final, six-week ROTC summer camp due to illness. His absence meant that he would not receive a reserve commission in the Army.

"This probably saved me from artillery battles in France and Germany during World War II," Gallagher said.

Active military service was not on his mind in 1936, when, with degree in hand, he headed off to New York City to start a career as a commercial photographer. Quickly he built quite a client base and his work came to the attention of Tom Maloney, the *U.S. Camera* editor and friend of Edward Steichen.

Gallagher hadn't heard about Steichen's unit when the war broke out and had started his own efforts to get into uniform, applying to be a public information officer with the Navy.

His application for commission was dated February 23, 1942, nearly a month after Steichen's acceptance into the service, but neither his military records nor personal writings show any knowledge that Steichen was looking for photographers at the time. In fact, Gallagher was himself initially turned away by the Navy when he applied to be a public information officer.

"I was told that as a magazine photographer—a photojournalist—I did not fit the Navy's requirements [for being a public information officer]," Gallagher wrote years later. "Naval officers were not permitted to carry umbrellas or packages or cameras and photography was an enlisted man's rating in the Navy."

Like Steichen, Gallagher had a Navy captain on his side. In Gallagher's case, it was Captain John Gingrich, who was the military aide to Assistant Secretary of the Navy James Forrestal.

That intervention got him into the Navy, but not in any unit approaching photography or public affairs. On March 21, 1942, his commission was approved and his orders cut, and what he got was an assignment to the Armed Guard as a gunnery officer in charge of gunnery crews on merchant ships.

That was dangerous work. German U-boats prowled the Atlantic and menaced Allied shipping. Gun-crew casualties were high; one-quarter to a third of officers who became Armed Guard commanders ended up having one or more ships shot out from under them during their sea tour.

"I reported for duty on April 23, 1942, at the Fargo Building in Boston, where we were given lectures on international law by Annapolis instructors and introduced to the guns we would be in charge of," Gallagher said.

"As I recall, many of my classmates had been university instructors or lawyers or had experience handling people, but didn't meet the Navy's traditional idea of what an officer should be. In short, we quickly got the idea we were expendable."

After five weeks of training, Gallagher was shipped to the Naval Amphibious Base in Little Creek, Virginia, a smaller base not far from the large operations base at Norfolk.

"We all got a little reminder of what we were facing the night we arrived. We watched a German sub sink a merchant ship in sight of the base," he said. "None of us actually saw the submarine, but it was pretty obvious what was happening."

Gallagher's first assignment as an Armed Guard commander was to take a detachment of six sailors to act as fire watches during the salvage of a loaded merchant ship that had struck a mine and gone aground off North Carolina.

A similar salvage just weeks before had ended in disaster when smoking sailors triggered massive fires on board a salvaged ship under tow to Norfolk. Gallagher's job—enforce a strict no-smoking policy anywhere near the ship.

"This fact didn't make me the most popular man on the job," Gallagher recalled. "Patching the 81-foot hole in the hull was the job of the civilian tug boat *Relief*. Assigned to the task was a huge Danish diver who, along with his helper, who we called the 'Brooklyn Arab,' would immediately light up after every dive."

Watching from a nearby rowboat, Gallagher would often have to remind the civilian diver and his helper that he had explicit orders to prohibit smoking on board or alongside the ship, a statement he often gave while inspecting the .32-caliber revolver issued him for the occasion.

"There were lots of curses and lots of complaints," he said. "But there was no smoking."

Gallagher was later assigned to lead a crew of twenty-four sailors sent to man the guns installed on the SS *Arlyn* that was soon to leave in Convoy SG-6 bound for Baffin Bay, Greenland. Their job was to deliver supplies to workers building U.S. military airfields.

The ship had four hundred tons of explosives along with some heavy equipment for grading runways along with other items of need. "We were delayed a few days to install a frozen food locker to be filled with steaks for the airfield workers," he said.

Life at sea for the U.S. Navy sailors on these ships was boring, but to Gallagher it was an opportunity. He had brought along his personal camera, a twin-lens Rollieflex, with plenty of film and all the chemicals necessary to set up his own darkroom. Soon the young ensign could be seen moving about the ship taking pictures of everything he saw.

Meanwhile the convoy moved very slowly, and by August 27 had made it only as far as the Strait of Belle Isle, between the Canadian provinces of Newfoundland and Labrador.

But lying in wait for them in the strait that night was a German U-517. A new, long-range submarine on her maiden deployment under the command of Kapitänleutnant Paul Hartwig, the U-boat had sunk her first victim, the troop transport SS *Chatham* earlier that same day—though strict radio silence had prevented the *Arlyn* from learning of the disaster and pending danger.

Near midnight, Hartwig unleashed a spray of three torpedoes at the slow-moving *Arlyn*. Two slammed into the aging merchant ship and a third barely missed. A Navy tanker, the USS *Laramie,* was also hit during the attack, but didn't go down.

Knowing the ship was carrying dynamite, the civilian members of the crew quickly abandoned ship, expecting a cataclysmic explosion to come at any moment.

This left Gallagher and his crew of twenty-four enlisted Navy sailors alone on the ship, which was sinking fast and would disappear beneath the waves just over an hour from the time she was hit.

Still, hoping to save the ship, Gallagher did a quick inspection and found the torpedoes had hit and destroyed the frozen meat locker but missed the dynamite in the hold. Still, the ship was filling fast with water, and seeing the

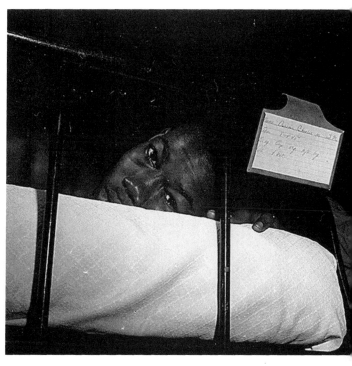

Seaman First Class Charlie Dunston, an amputee undergoing treatment at the Naval Hospital in Philadelphia, Pennsylvania, August 1, 1945.

situation was hopeless, he prepared his sailors to enter the cold, icy water.

"I told my Armed Guard crew there would be a strong current in the strait," Gallagher said. "We would go in the water together, swim with the current and search for life rafts."

Staying together saved the sailors, but thirteen of the merchant crew ended up missing and were presumed to have either gone down with the ship or perished at sea afterward.

Gradually, Gallagher and his men found life rafts and even a lifeboat and pulled themselves aboard.

"We soon noticed a sweeping searchlight combing the waters and I immediately ordered my men to stay low in their boats or in the water," Gallagher said. "It was the German sub looking for survivors for machinegun practice."

By dawn, Gallagher and his crew were picked up by the tugboat *Relief,* the same boat that had been the scene of his no-smoking commands just weeks before.

"It was the same Danish diver who pulled me onto the deck and immediately recognized me through a coating of fuel oil," Gallagher remembered. "All I remember is him yelling to the rest of the crew that 'it's the goddamned ensign—throw him back!'"

Gallagher brought back every one of his men and arrived in Boston catching rides first on the Coast Guard cutter *Mojave* and later on the patched-up oiler *Laramie*.

In Boston, Naval Intelligence debriefed his crew before sending them all on to Brooklyn to await assignment to another Armed Guard crew.

It was there that Gallagher got some bad news. While in Armed Guard school, he'd heard the Navy wanted to bring in photographic officers for duty on board carriers and he'd applied to be considered for a switch to the aviation community. In the end it was the "needs of the Navy" that won out and Gallagher was turned down by the Navy's personnel juggernaut at the Bureau of Navigation. Due to a shortage of qualified officers in the Armed Guard, his rejection letter read, "the bureau regrets that favorable consideration cannot be given."

This meant Gallagher's adventures riding merchant ships would continue for most of the next year as he made a five-month voyage on the new merchant ship *Cape Henlopen*. The ship headed out from New York in 1942 on the way to Egypt—the long way. This meant down around the Cape of Good Hope and up through the Indian Ocean to the Suez Canal.

Again Gallagher would spend time off watch taking photographs. The images show the Armed Guard life at sea, but aren't in the official government collection and few have seen the light of day. Today, these images rest in the collection of the Cornell University Library and not in the National Archives, because Gallagher was not an "official" Navy photographer at the time and was under no obligation to give the government his work.

Returning to Norfolk was no small feat, either. Because of the U-boat threat, the ship went back south and around Africa across the South Atlantic—up the west coast of South America to the Panama Canal. Once through the canal, she joined a convoy for Norfolk.

In all it was a five-month journey, but their luck nearly turned bad during the final approach to Norfolk. Leaving her convoy, she headed for Norfolk the evening of March 27, 1943, and ran head-on into the SS *Lillian Luckenbach,* a freighter heading out of Norfolk.

"The *Luckenbach* sank with one of the *Cape Henlopen*'s anchors in her hold," Gallagher would later recall. "When dawn came, we found ourselves five miles off Virginia Beach, but a fire had turned the deckplates in the bow red hot, exposing the ammunition magazines to excessive heat.

"I had the gunner's mate hand each shell carefully up to me on deck and I, in turn, tossed each over the side—I later had to account for a considerable amount of dumped ammunition to the Naval Ammunition Depot, but once they heard the complete story, there were no complaints."

The rest of the trip into Norfolk was uneventful.

After surviving a year in the Armed Guard, Gallagher and a number of other officers were transferred to duty on destroyer escorts as gunnery officers. En route to their new commands, each received more schooling in the use of the new five-inch guns and fire-control techniques as well as submarine-chasing techniques and shipboard firefighting.

It was mid-1943 when Gallagher received orders to join the crew of the newly built USS *John J. Powers* as the ship's first assistant gunnery officer. Around that time, he also heard about Steichen's unit and their mission to document naval aviation.

While in New York for fitting out on the *Powers,* Gallagher had met Steichen through *U.S. Camera* editor Tom Maloney.

Hearing his qualifications, Steichen offered Gallagher a billet. But knowing there was a shortage of gunnery officers, this time Gallagher turned down the orders and chose to help fight the battle of the Atlantic instead.

"We spent most of the time I was on board in Atlantic convoy duty," Gallagher said. "These were small ships and it was nothing for them to roll forty-

Japanese soldiers who gave themselves up at Kerama-retto on board U.S. Navy ship in May 1945.

U.S. Marines walk down a flight line on Falalop Island, Ulithi Atoll, in December 1944.

five degrees every eight or nine seconds." To stay in his bunk, Gallagher had to wedge himself in with laundry baskets.

"Between watch-standing duties and all the compulsory training we had to conduct regularly, not to mention alerts that could come at anytime," he would recall, "sleep on board was fragmented into small pieces, seized whenever available."

In the end, Gallagher made two cruises across the Atlantic and impressed his commanding officer, Lieutenant Commander E. Allen Loew, with his performance as the ship's assistant gunnery officer.

On board the *Powers,* Gallagher was promoted to lieutenant and received the blessing of Loew, who deemed him qualified to be the gunnery officer as well as a fully qualified officer of the deck, capable of handling the ship while under way.

But it wasn't lost on Loew that Gallagher had other talents the Navy could make use of during the war. In his final fitness report from the *Powers* on September 19, 1944—just as the ship was to depart for her third convoy across the Atlantic—Loew wrote: "Lt. Gallagher is a contentious, industrious and intelligent officer who has special qualifications as a professional photographer. He has long desired to enter photographic work in the Navy, but wished to qualify as a sea-going deck officer first—this he has done well.

"It is this officer's opinion that he is in a position to render service in the photographic field that could not be produced by a man qualified only as a professional photographer."

Loew's words about Gallagher's unique qualifications would prove to be prophetic. Leaving the *Powers* with mixed emotions, Gallagher collected his official government camera gear and headed west to cover the war in the Pacific as one of Steichen's boys.

While Gallagher was quite a catch for the Steichen unit, other officers joined the unit as well. Charles Steinheimer, who had been working for *Life* magazine during the early years of the war, put on a uniform and ended up as the photographic officer on two aircraft carriers, though he also produced some images of his own.

Another catch for Steichen was John Swope, a Hollywood special-effects photographer.

Before the war, Swope began his military career in the Army Air Corps as a flight instructor, but officials soon learned of his photographic skills and he was teamed up with author John Steinbeck to produce the book *Bombs Away,* a revealing documentary of the air corps pilot training program.

At Steichen's request and with his help, Swope was able to transfer his commission to the Navy, where he became an asset to Steichen's motion picture crew, headed up by Lieutenant Commander Dwight Long.

Even Wayne Miller, now an experienced lieutenant, was able to help recruit fresh blood into the unit, and a school colleague of his from his days at the Art Institute in Los Angeles, Ensign Tomas Binford, joined the unit and headed to the Pacific.

In a final stroke of genius, Steichen was able to wrestle First Lieutenant Paul Dorsey away from the U.S. Marine Corps. Dorsey's images of amphibious landings in the Pacific would provide the Steichen unit with battle images from the front.

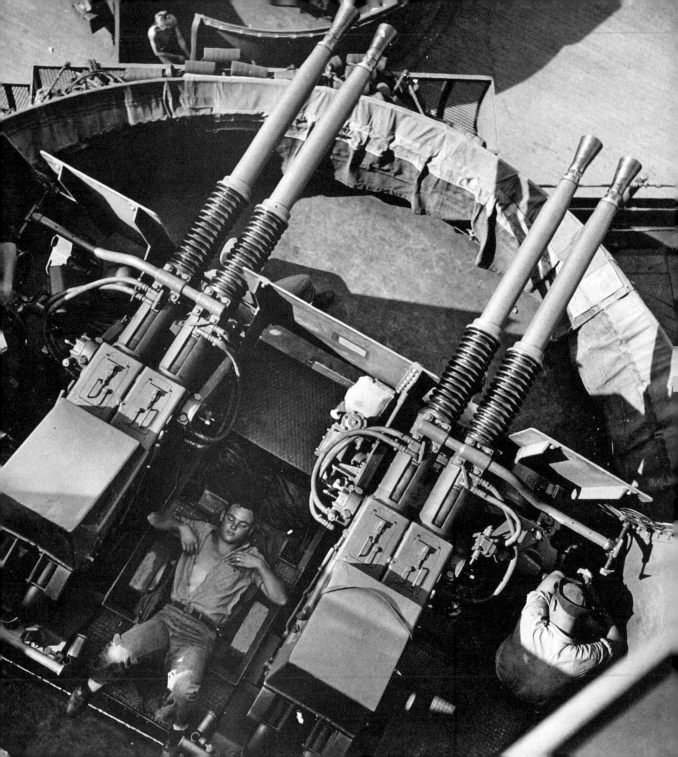

CHAPTER 7

1944:
The War Continues

✯　　✯　　✯

WHILE IN WASHINGTON between assignments, Miller recalled Steichen never micromanaged his shooters. Instead, he allowed them to pursue their own paths and ideas, gently steering them along the way.

"He never really gave much guidance though he'd help if you asked—we were free to pursue our own stories," Miller said. "That, in turn, gave us the tremendous responsibility of coming back with something, but he had this faith in us and it paid off."

Steichen coached his photographers to shoot what they wanted to shoot most of the time, but to make sure they also took the stock pictures—the standard shots the brass was expecting of men, ships, and aircraft at war.

"I remember one time he said, 'I don't care what you do, Wayne,'" Miller recalls Steichen telling him during one of the young photographer's Washington stops. "You must keep in your mind the necessity to bring back something that will please the brass, but spend the rest of your time photographing the man; the little guy; the guts, the heartaches, the struggle, plus the dreams and frustrations of this little guy—this sailor."

By this time in the war, there wasn't much Stateside shooting for the unit anymore. Jorgensen made a quick trip to New York in February of 1944 to photograph an experimental helicopter before heading back to the Pacific and carrier duty on the escort carrier *Monterey*.

PREVIOUS PAGE: *A sailor catches up on sleep between twin 40mm anti-aircraft guns on board the battleship* New Jersey *in December 1944.*

Arriving on the ship in late May, Jorgensen participated in aerial raids on the Marianas Islands, the invasion of Guam, as well as the Battle of the Philippine Sea. He flew in combat, netting his second battle star for his combat aircrew wings.

He also spent time wandering about the ship, capturing other images of life on board. He photographed crew members playing basketball on an elevator in the ship's hangar. Two sailors are reaching for the jump ball. One of those sailors was then Lieutenant Gerald R. Ford—the future president of the United States.

Though the picture got some play at the time, the image resurfaced, getting even more play, during Ford's time as vice president and later president in the mid-1970s.

A game of basketball is played on the aircraft elevator of the escort aircraft carrier Monterey *during operations in the Marianas Islands against Saipan and Guam. The blond sailor at the left is Lieutenant Gerald R. Ford, who would later become the thirty-eighth president of the United States.*

BACKGROUND: *An aerial view of the Invasion of Guam on July 21, 1944, taken by Lieutenant Victor Jorgensen flying off the carrier Monterey, which was supporting the invasion with close air support for the troops on the beach.*

Lieutenant Fenno Jacobs left the relative comfort of ships at sea to live in the dust with the Navy's only land-based fighter squadron—Fighter Squadron 17, led by Commander Tom Blackburn, who had formerly led the fighter squadron on the *Santee* when Bristol had been on board for the invasion of North Africa.

Seeking to create a sense of esprit de corps, Blackburn had dubbed his squadron the "Jolly Rogers" and adopted a skull-and-crossbones insignia as their squadron flag and patch.

Ensign Robert Zemke is greeted by a reception committee after making the five hundredth arrested landing on the escort carrier Monterey *during the Marianas operations in July 1944.*

Living and competing with Marine Corps fighter squadrons, Blackburn's men were the Navy's version of Major Gregg "Pappy" Boyington and his Marine "Black Sheep."

The squadron was forced off fleet carriers and onto an airstrip on the now-secure island of Bougainville. The Jolly Rogers operated from a dirt strip they shared with a Marine squadron—though not Boyington's.

The reason for their exile was the squadron's aircraft; the gull-winged F4U Corsair had been temporarily dubbed too unstable to land on carriers.

A sailor peers over the rim of a gun tub on board the battleship New Jersey, *as the ship's forward smokestack looms in the background. The ship was engaged in combat operations near the Philippine Islands in December 1944.*

Blackburn would eventually be key to the Navy's final acceptance of the Corsair as a carrier-based aircraft through the end of the war, but that was in the future.

Jacobs had left Washington in January and spent time in Hawaii, where he documented pilots on rest and relaxation at special "rest homes" where they were provided beaches, food, drink, and even female companionship while on short leaves from the war zones. A similar facility was photographed by Bristol in New Zealand.

It would be near the end of his trip that Jacobs caught up with Blackburn and company on Bougainville.

Though he adequately captured the squadron's life and activities on the ground, there's no photographic evidence that he flew any missions, as no aerial photographs of the squadron from Jacobs exist in the National Archives from his time with VF-17. Still, it is most likely that he did fly missions, as other unit members did when attached to flying units for extended periods.

The most likely explanation for this absence is that none of his images passed security reviews and remained classified after the war.

Classified missions were also part of Bristol's life during 1944. He had headed to the South Pacific and was using his old Alaska connections in the Navy's patrol to fly on reconnaissance and rescue missions behind enemy lines.

Here, Bristol would take one of his most famous pictures of the war—of a naked sailor in the blister gunner's bubble in the side of a PBY Catalina patrol aircraft. The sequence shows the young sailor taking off his clothes to jump into the water to rescue a pilot who had become blind when he was shot down.

Flying boats, along with submarines, were the primary weapons the U.S. military used to rescue pilots from behind enemy lines. Bristol's gunner picture is part of a sequence of images that documents one of the six "dumbo" rescue missions he took part in while operating in the waters off Rabaul, St. Georges Channel, and Duke of York Island in the Solomon Islands.

But no photographic evidence exists of his participation in the two-night "blackcat" reconnaissance missions near Bougainville or two long-range search missions over "hot" enemy-held islands. Commander G. R. Henderson, however, who was then head of Fleet Air Wing 1, reported favorably on Bristol's conduct on the missions to the Bureau of Aeronautics for inclusion in his fitness report.

"Some of his data and photographs are probably of such a nature that security will not permit release at this time," Henderson wrote of Bristol's work.

OPPOSITE: *An officer spends his free time in his stateroom on board the battleship* New Jersey *playing an accordion while the ship was en route to the Philippines. Note the family photos on the safe in the background.*

"It is hoped that as much of his data as can be released be published in national news periodicals for the definite morale effect his fine work will have on the flight personnel concerned."

Henderson also put Bristol in for an Air Medal, which he was finally awarded after the war's end.

The unit had no one at the momentous D-day landings in June of 1944, as the Allies began to take back Europe. But soon thereafter, Miller made one of the unit's rare deployments to the Mediterranean and the Atlantic theater of operations.

A gunner's mate cleans inside the massive sixteen-inch gun barrels on board the battleship New Jersey *en route to the Philippines.*

On June 27, 1944, Miller left Quonset Point Naval Air Station on board the escort carrier *Tulagi*, bound for Europe and the invasion of southern France. On August 15, he flew high over the beaches to document the invasion, which went on unopposed at first.

Miller left the *Tulagi* on August 18 for Bastia, Corsica, where he joined Fighter Squadron 74 at the Ajaccio airstrip. The pilots of the squadron were flying night-fighter missions over the invasion force in specially designed aircraft and sleeping during the day.

Miller captured the unit both on and off duty, including tastefully done skinny-dipping sailors swimming in a Corsican lake. He stayed with the unit until September 5, then headed first to Naples for a few days, where he awaited a flight to Casablanca, and then back to the

Ensign Andrew Jagger of Southampton, New York, of Fighter Squadron 17 describes an aerial dogfight he won to Lieutenant H. A. March of Washington, D.C., in February 1944, when the squadron was based at the Piva Airstrip on the Island of Bougainville in the South Pacific.

States. For a few days, Miller was able to wander about the city, photographing street children—a welcome break from covering the men and machines and events of war.

Once back in D.C., Miller spent two weeks with Steichen before heading to New York.

Gradually, the unit's center of operations was moving from D.C. to New York City, and home base was now becoming the Literature Division of the Special Services Depot located at 1 Park Place in downtown Manhattan.

Pilots from Navy Fighter Squadron 17 get an intelligence briefing prior to getting ready for a mission in February 1944. Seated in the center with his cap on is Squadron Commander John T. Blackburn. The squadron was land-based on Bougainville in the South Pacific.

Even Steichen would often escape D.C. to work out of the New York office, which gave him a chance to get home to Connecticut once in a while.

Jacobs spent the rest of 1944 mostly hopping from carrier to carrier in the Pacific. But in November, he got the chance to take a ride on the battleship *New Jersey*.

It was here that Jacob's talent shined the brightest. As was the case in his photographs of aircraft factories in 1943, Jacobs's strength seemed to be in showing man inside glorious monuments of industry, juxtaposing the human element with the massive machinery of the battleship *New Jersey*, as seen in his

Lieutenant Commander John T. Blackburn, commanding officer of Fighter Squadron 17, stands in front of his squadron's "scoreboard" identifying the number of Japanese aircraft his fliers had shot down. The image was taken in February 1944 when the squadron was based at the Piva Airstrip on the Island of Bougainville in the South Pacific.

shots of crew members in and around the ship's stacks or his shot from above of a sailor sleeping between barrels in a 40mm gun tub.

He also found time to take some tender images, for example the one in which a sailor works on the tattoo of a shipmate, which many consider a classic representation of the closeness that develops among a ship's crew.

As often happened with unit members, while Jacobs lived and worked from the *New Jersey,* newcomer Barrett Gallagher, fresh from duty as the gunnery officer on board a destroyer escort, joined Admiral Gerald Bogan's staff on the carrier *Intrepid,* the two boats just a few miles away to starboard or port on most days.

Shortly after noon on November 25, a heavy force of Japanese planes struck at the *Intrepid* and her task force. Within five minutes, two kamikazes crashed into the carrier, killing six officers and five sailors.

Having spent the whole war at sea and having been under enemy fire before, Gallagher managed to photograph some in the aftermath of the kamikaze attack that left the *Intrepid* ablaze and trailing smoke. Jacobs caught the same scene from the nearby *New Jersey*.

On board the *Intrepid,* Gallagher had been photographing flight-deck operations when the suicide aircraft hit. After firing off a few frames, the former destroyer sailor put down the cameras and became just one of the crew—though he was not ship's company.

"Lieutenant Gallagher voluntarily assisted in the removal of casualties and, despite the constant menace of exploding ammunition and spreading flames, subsequently manned a hose, gallantly fighting the fires raging on both flight and gallery decks," reads Gallagher's Bronze Star medal—with a V device for valor—awarded to him for his actions on board the *Intrepid* that day.

Because of the actions of the crew, the *Intrepid* never lost propulsion or left her station in the task group, and in less than two hours, the last blaze had

Fenno Jacobs spent time at the Chris Holmes Rest Home in February 1944 where Navy pilots on leave from combat relaxed and enjoyed. In one image, fingers replace forks at chow-time while in another one a couple dances while another relaxes on the side. Hawaii, March 1944.

been extinguished. The next day, Gallagher resumed his photography during the burial at sea of the eleven who died in the attack. His shutter caught the bodies as they slipped off the stretchers and into the water—an image published over and over during the final days of the war.

Ceremony over, the *Intrepid* left immediately for San Francisco for repairs, while Gallagher and the rest of Bogan's staff transferred to the aircraft carrier *Lexington* to continue operations.

The *New Jersey* sailed with the *Lexington* task group for air attacks on Luzon in mid-December. Then Jacobs and the ship's crew were caught in a typhoon in which three destroyers just disappeared without a trace.

But her size and the experience of the *New Jersey*'s crew brought the battleship into the fleet's base at Ulithi in the Caroline Islands on Christmas Eve. There, she was met by Fleet Admiral Chester W. Nimitz, who came on board to confer with Halsey—an event Jacobs captured on film.

Jacobs spent this time photographing the men and officers as they took breaks at the atoll's recreation center. Jacobs stayed with the ship until the end of January when he would head back to the United States for a break of his own.

In September 1944, Steichen wrote a memo to Admiral Radford highlighting the unit's progress since its formation in 1942. Over eleven-thousand selected black-and-white and almost three-thousand color photographs were

PT boats speed back to base after a successful mission to insert members of the U.S. Army's 1st Battalion, 305th Infantry behind enemy lines to take the town of Palompon on Leyte in the Philippine Islands, Christmas Day, 1944.

Firefighters extinguish dozens of small fires burning on the carrier Intrepid's *flight deck on November 25, 1944, in the inferno that followed her being hit. It was the worst day in the history of the ship, when two kamikaze planes hit the ship within five minutes of each another, killing sixty-nine and seriously wounding eight-five. Gallagher was himself in the thick of it, putting down the cameras and leading hose teams—for which he was awarded the Bronze Star medal with V device for valor.*

Sergeant J. S. Wilson, U.S. Army, painting a pretty female design on nose of a bomber based at Eniwetok Island in the South Pacific, in June 1944. Though Navy, none of Steichen's photographers failed to photograph any "target of opportunity" from any service.

Pilots slip into flight gear aboard the Essex-class carrier USS Ticonderoga *for strike on Manila, Philippine Islands, on November 5, 1944.*

in the unit's collections in Washington. Steichen began to lobby the Navy to maintain his unit's work in a separate collection from the rest of the Navy's public-relations and intelligence photography.

He also began planning a new photographic exhibition along the lines of *The Road to Victory.* It was set to open in January 1945 at the Museum of Modern Art in New York.

Part of the collection was the motion-picture work that Lieutenant Dwight Long had been doing on the *Yorktown* and other carriers around the fleet, work that was now getting Hollywood's attention.

Steichen traveled to Rochester, New York, on November 19, 1944, to address the Technical Section of the Professional Photographers of America and show film clips that would become part of a soon-to-be-released, hour-long documentary film, *The Fighting Lady.*

The complete movie would premier in December 1944 in Los Angeles and be shown in New York in January of 1945.

Steichen's role in the filming and editing was minimal, though his record shows two trips to Los Angeles, where he served as a "technical advisor" and participated in the editing work being headed up by Louis de Rochemont of 20th Century Fox Pictures. Actor Robert Taylor narrated the film.

The movie won an Academy Award for documentary film in early 1945. Most impressive were the film's aerial combat scenes, which had been masterminded by Long, who placed movie cameras in the aircrafts' wings next to the machine guns. This innovation gave audiences a view they'd not seen before—the view from the cockpit.

Black sailors in their bunkroom aboard the Essex-class aircraft carrier Ticonderoga *on eve of the Battle of Manila, Philippine Islands. Steward's Mate First Class Thomas L. Crenshaw (on bunk) looks at a picture of his three children, while a bunkmate writes a letter home, Novemer 4, 1944.*

Japanese prisoners of war bathe each other, have their heads shaved, and are deloused after being taken on board the battleship New Jersey, *while a great portion of the crew look on. The Japanese sailors had been in a small vessel spying on the* New Jersey.

Gunner's mates in the barbette of the ship's massive sixteen-inch guns prepare to ram large bags of gunpowder into the breach of one of the guns— enough powder to send the gun's 2,700-pound projectile up to twenty-four miles.

A sailor writes home after mail call on board the battleship New Jersey *operating in the South Pacific in December 1944.*

It is often said a sailor can sleep anywhere, as this young sailor shows sleeping just inside a hatch on board the battleship New Jersey *while en route to the Philippines in December 1944.*

True shipmates: a sailor works on a tattoo for a friend during an off moment at sea on board the battleship New Jersey *in the South Pacific in December 1944.*

One sailor plays the trumpet while another sings during after hours in their berthing area on board the battleship New Jersey *in the South Pacific.*

The crew of the PT-190 pose in front of a broom they displayed to tell everyone they had a successful patrol—a "clean sweep."

One of Gallagher's most famous photos of the war taken on November 26, 1944, the day after two kamikaze aircraft hit the Intrepid within five minutes of each other, killing sixty-nine and wounding another eight-five. Here the sailors' shipmates prepare to send the dead into the ocean in a time-honored burial-at-sea ceremony.

CHAPTER 8

1945:
The Push to Tokyo

✯   ✯   ✯

IN 1945, STEICHEN learned he'd been promoted to captain and he would now no longer just command the Aviation Photographic Unit, but all Navy combat photography in the Pacific.

His exhibit *Power in the Pacific* opened at the Museum of Modern Art in New York on January 24, 1945. In addition to Steichen's unit, it featured Marine and Coast Guard as well as other Navy combat photography.

The exhibition was intended to be a recapitulation of the war in the Pacific as seen through the camera's lens and the photographer's eye. *Power in the Pacific* reworked the ideas Steichen had pioneered in the earlier *The Road to Victory,* with photographs of various sizes organized in a way that guided the reader through the exhibit.

Lieutenant Roark Bradford, a poet on duty with the Navy, was assigned to write the accompanying text just as Steichen's brother-in-law Carl Sandburg had been assigned to *The Road to Victory.*

According to photographic historian Chris Phillips, Lieutenant George Kidder Smith was brought in to design the exhibition. Smith, who was an architect and photographer, had worked with the Museum of Modern Art before the war.

He remembers his time with Steichen on the project as being "an enormous amount of stimulating fun . . . At one point the Captain and I had a longstanding disagreement as to which photograph should lead off the show," Phillips quotes Smith as saying.

PREVIOUS PAGE: *Seaman Paul Gray of San Dimus, California, rides a Japanese bicycle on the streets of Tokyo shortly after the Japanese surrendered.*

"He wanted, no, he was insistent on a six by eight foot panel showing the 16 inch guns of an Iowa class battleship firing. I did not think that this symbolized 'man' enough and mulled on what could be used for weeks until I found a great shot, one shot by Victor Jorgensen of a deck full of cheering sailors."

Getting his courage together, Smith approached Steichen with his new idea. "I said to the Captain that I thought that this would 'key' the show better than the firing guns."

"Kidder, you are absolutely right," Steichen replied, surprising everyone in the room.

"He was that kind of person: brilliant, demanding to the millimeter, contagiously enthusiastic, and always receptive to the ideas of others," Smith said.

The Washington lab was not equipped to print the largest murals needed for the show, but that didn't stop Steichen.

Camera repairman Marty Forscher said the largest of the prints were processed on the photo lab floor by barefoot technicians who used mops laden with developer and later fixer to make the photographs permanent. The finished prints were rushed to New York for retouching and mounting.

Power in the Pacific was another great success for the museum. Like *The Road to Victory*, it moved to other locations, making stops at the Corcoran Gallery in Washington, the Massachusetts Institute of Technology, Yale University, and

U.S. Pacific submarine on war patrol. Pacific sunlight silvers the sea, July 1945.

A Navy Curtiss Helldiver (SB2C) is snapped against the background provided by its carrier as it returns from a strike at Japanese shipping. Far below, other planes are being spotted on the flight deck to which the SB2C will soon return, January 1945.

Task Force 58 raid on Japan. 40mm guns firing aboard USS Hornet on February 16, 1945, as the carrier's planes were raiding Tokyo. Note expended shells and ready-service ammunition at right.

Navy personnel on liberty at Mogmog Island. Enlisted men lounge about a tiny island with plenty of beer, November 1944.

USS Sea Dog *prowls the Pacific in search of enemy shipping, May 19, 1945.*

the Minnesota Institute of Fine Arts. In addition, the photographs in the show were reproduced in a paperback book and can still be found in many libraries.

Meanwhile, out in the Pacific, the war raged on. Unit members Bristol, Kerlee, and Gallagher were all present during the invasion of Iwo Jima, operating from different carriers. Gallagher and Jorgensen would be present at Okinawa as well.

Now in charge of all combat photography, Captain Steichen decided to make another trip into the war zone and headed to Guam in March to see firsthand how it was being done "in the field."

On Guam, he met up with Kerlee, who photographed him among native children between tours of the island's military and photographic facilities and talking to the hundreds of sailors now under his charge.

He and Kerlee even had a special officers' club lunch with famed reporter Ernie Pyle, who would die less than a month later on Okinawa. But Steichen wanted to get closer to the action and caught an airplane to Iwo Jima, arriving the day after U.S. officials declared the island secure.

Steichen's friend Tom Maloney, an Annapolis graduate, had been unable to get a Navy commission in the early days of the war after he had been injured in an automobile accident, but now he gave up his editor's hat and became *U.S. Camera*'s war correspondent, allowing him to photograph the war from close up.

He met Steichen in Guam, and the two old friends, along with Steichen's administrative assistant, Lieutenant Willard Mace, left for a tour of the island's

Guam, March 9, 1945: Captain Edward Steichen, Ernie Pyle and Lieutenant Commander Charles Kerlee enjoy lunch at the officers' club on the island of Guam. March 9, 1945.

battlegrounds. They landed on Iwo Jima even as the Marines were still mopping up and rooting out the remaining Japanese defenders.

Iwo Jima, March 1944: With fighting still going on in parts of the island, Captain Edward Steichen views the devastation the island has suffered with his eyes and camera along with war correspondent and friend Tom Maloney, the editor of U.S. Camera Magazine, and an unidentified Marine Corps guard.

Iwo Jima, March 1944: Captain Edward Steichen, along with war correspondent and friend Tom Maloney, the editor of U.S. Camera Magazine, take a peek inside the wreckage of a bombed-out landing craft on one of the island's beaches.

While on Iwo, Steichen produced over ninety photographs, a number of which were published along with a text he wrote a few months later.

His images show destroyed landing craft abandoned on the black beaches, airplane fragments embedded in rubble, and the "desolate mass of rocks, steel, and tangled vegetation."

But among his favorite images were two contrasting shots he claimed would show the horror of war and the promise of peace. The first image is that of the fingers of a dead Japanese soldier poking up through the dirt. Not far away, he photographed a white flower trying to poke through the war's destruction as a kind of symbol of rebirth. The images were published side by side in *U.S. Camera* a few months later.

On his first night on the island, Steichen got a real taste of just how close he was to the war and personal danger.

ABOVE AND OPPOSITE: *March 1944: With fighting still going on in parts of the island, Captain Edward Steichen took this photo, part of a two-image series he said showed the horrors of war and the promise of the coming peace. This photo shows a new flower blooming through the wreckage of trees and rocks thrown around by the explosions of war. The second photo, by contrast, shows the fingers of a dead Japanese soldier peeking through the rubble that buried and killed him.*

"A number of fliers who had arrived the same day as [I] were killed by Japanese soldiers who came out from hiding places to drop hand grenades into the tents of the sleeping men," he said.

Steichen biographer Penelope Niven wrote that the events on Iwo Jima were "a horrible finale for Steichen's close-up of the war . . . the carnage haunted him, further hardening his resolve to turn images of war into instruments of peace."

His appointment as head of the Navy's combat photography coincided with his being named the director of the newly created Naval Photographic Insti-

tute, based at the Naval Photographic Center on the Anacostia Naval Air Station in Washington, D.C. The organization didn't last long, quietly disappearing when the service began its massive demobilization after the war, and there is no surviving document describing the institute or its formal mission.

Its last official act was to hold an awards banquet at which the top photography from all the sea services was honored. This was held on October 27, 1945. Every member of Steichen's original unit was honored with a citation, including many of the enlisted shooters, along with Coast Guard, Marine, and other Navy combat photographers from around the world.

Most of the photographers stayed in the field during the final days of the war, periodically stopping by New York and Washington to recharge and to process film before heading out again into the fray.

Both Wayne Miller and Fenno Jacobs happened to be in Washington on April 12, 1945, when Franklin Roosevelt's sudden death in Warm Springs, Georgia, plunged the nation into mourning. The two documented the events and reactions of the people in Washington as Roosevelt's body was brought through the capital. Instead of shooting the caisson with Roosevelt's flag-draped coffin, Miller photographed the mourning public, catching their facial expressions as the casket passed by.

Miller followed Roosevelt's body all the way to Hyde Park, New York, for the final burial, photographing the lonely casket sitting half buried in the ground.

By the beginning of May, Kerlee applied for an early release from the service for hardship reasons. His wife, Claire, had become despondent during the photographer's long absences in the war zones and the problem was only getting worse, threatening the mental health of both members of the couple along with their marriage.

"During the past 20 months, I have undergone severe nervous strain due to the neurotic condition of my wife," he wrote in his request to be put on inactive duty. "The basic cause for her condition was our continued separation."

OPPOSITE: *A nation's sorrow at the loss of President Franklin D. Roosevelt is reflected in the faces of thousands who lined the streets of Washington, D.C. during his funeral, April 14, 1945.*

He had tried to keep Claire busy, first in 1944, by having her join the Women's Army Corps, but that didn't work and she was discharged less than twelve months later for psychiatric reasons.

"It is my definite impression that unless you can devote considerable time and attention to the marriage, the situation will quickly become utterly hopeless," wrote Dr. Donald Power Wilson, a Los Angeles psychologist who had been working with Claire for over a year. "If this eventuality should occur, I would be very apprehensive of her nervous and emotional state."

Wilson went on to advise Kerlee to resign his commission, return home to his wife, and try to patch things up, easing the nervous strain on both. Kerlee himself, now a Lieutenant Commander, was beginning to crack under the strain, a fact that was noted in his fitness reports.

The application slowly worked its way through the Navy's bureaucracy, being approved at all the necessary levels, but on July 28, Kerlee learned that the Bureau of Personnel had rejected his request.

Gallagher continued to travel with Admiral Bogan and saw action off Okinawa. Eventually, he received an Air Medal for "participating in aerial flights in operations against the enemy in the vicinity of the Philippine Islands, Nansei Shoto and Honshu."

At the same time, Jorgensen went aboard the hospital ship *Solace* and arrived off the Japanese-held island of Okinawa on the morning of March 27, the second day of the battle.

Immediately patients were brought on board from various ships. Jorgensen would spend a month on the *Solace* as she ferried the wounded back to Guam. His images of wounded soldiers, sailors, and Marines undergoing treatment on the hospital ship were widely reproduced in both Navy and civilian publications.

Still in early May 1945, Victor Jorgensen arrived in the Philippines on board the destroyer *Albert W. Grant* in time to witness the streets of Manila slowly

OPPOSITE: *Casualties from Okinawa are brought on board the hospital ship* Solace *from landing craft that brought them out from the island.*

returning to life. He photographed sailors on liberty in the bombed-out town and ships tied up in the harbor.

The *Grant* left Manila on June 3, escorting General Douglas MacArthur, on board the cruiser *Boise,* on a tour of the Philippines.

The *Grant* then sailed southwest toward Brunei Bay, Borneo, where Jorgensen photographed the Australian and British landings on June 10. He left the ship on June 15, after it arrived back in Manila, and headed back to the United States, arriving in early July.

Sailors from the destroyer Albert W. Grant *plot targets for the gun crews as they shell enemy positions during landings at Brunei Bay, Borneo, June 10, 1945.*

Opposite page: *The bow of the destroyer* Albert W. Grant *as the ship lies at anchor in Manila Harbor, Philippines, in June 1945.*

Jorgensen was working in the New York offices of the Steichen unit on August 14 when the announcement of the Japanese surrender came. He photographed the nightlong celebrations of millions in the streets of Manhattan.

He was only a few feet away from legendary *Life* photographer Alfred Eisenstadt, who captured a sailor kissing a nurse in Times Square. Jorgensen captured the same moment, but with a different background. Eisenstadt's view shows more of Times Square in the background, while Jorgensen's image shows the two kissing in front of a building.

It is Jorgensen's image rather than Eisenstadt's that is often used today, the copyright of the latter still being owned by *Life*. Jorgensen's image is in the public domain, meaning it was produced with tax dollars and therefore available for use by all.

Barrett Gallagher was hard at work, making up for lost photographic time early in the war; he would be one of the last two Steichen unit members to return home from the war.

After the Japanese surrender, Admiral William Halsey ordered the entire Third Fleet to assemble for an hour-long photo exercise called "Operation

Snapshot." It was Gallagher who spent the time aloft photographing more than five thousand vessels making turns in formation off Japan; the planes in these images are sometimes misconstrued as being an invasion fleet.

On September 2, 1945, Gallagher was on board Halsey's flagship, the USS *Missouri*, for the formal signing of the surrender documents announcing the end of the war.

But it was Miller, the unit's youngest member, who would have the final adven-

Japanese envoys leave the USS Missouri *(BB-63) in Tokyo Bay, Japan, after signing surrender papers, September 2, 1945.*

Discharged Japanese soldiers in Horoshima, Japan, share a light for their cigarettes as they take advantage of free transportation home in September 1945, after the formal Japanese surrender.

ture of the war. After news of the Japanese surrender, he boarded the attack transport *Braxton* in Guam and went to Japan, where she delivered the first occupation troops on August 30.

Miller went ashore to document the occupation troops taking control of Japanese facilities. Defying orders, he and a civilian correspondent from *Time* magazine caught a train in an attempt to get to Hiroshima to document the atomic-bomb damage.

In every town he passed on his way south, Miller saw soldiers waiting for trains and made many images of these Japanese warriors trying to make their way home.

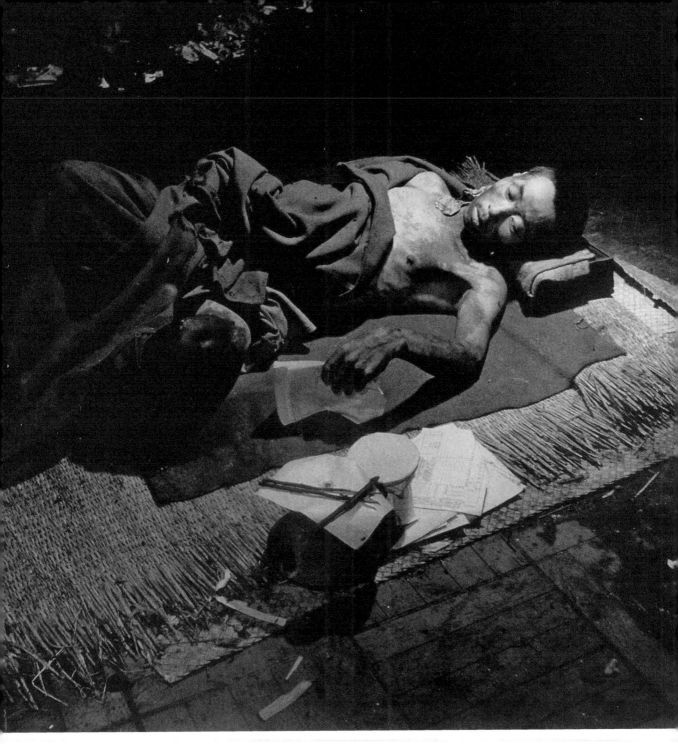

A victim of the atomic blast in Hiroshima, Japan, lies in a makeshift hospital made out of a bank building.

A Japanese soldier walks through a leveled area of Hiroshima that was destroyed by the atomic bomb just days before.

Arriving in Hiroshima, Miller walked around the devastation, photographing a lone soldier walking among the rubble as well as documenting the wounded and those who lay dying from exposure to radiation. He stayed only long enough to document the horror, but the impact of that time has remained with him to this day.

A rubble-covered area of Hiroshima illustrates the damage caused by the atomic bomb blast.

"I was not prepared for the horrors we saw in Hiroshima," Miller recalled. "The devastation was the ultimate denial of sanity and not something I will ever forget."

Making his way back to Tokyo, Miller located and photographed many former American prisoners of war before rejoining the *Braxton* on September 1, when the ship left Tokyo Harbor, bound for Saipan.

Miller spent the next couple of weeks working his way back across the Pacific, finally arriving in Washington D. C. on September 24. Gallagher would follow him back to the States a few weeks later.

The Essex-class aircraft carrier Lexington *refuels from a Navy tanker in the China Sea.*

Kerlee's request for a release from active duty, denied in July, was approved on August 17, and he became the first Steichen unit member to return to civilian life.

Most of the unit had spent so much time overseas that they had no problem qualifying for release as well, and most were discharged by Thanksgiving. Steichen himself left active duty on October 22, but stuck around Washington for the Naval Photographic Institute awards ceremony, held on October 25, at the National Press Club in Washington, coinciding with an exhibit there of 150 prints.

On November 6, Secretary of the Navy James Forrestal awarded Steichen the Navy's Distinguished Service Medal. He had been recommended for the

Legion of Merit, lower in level of merit than the DSM, by Admiral Mark Mitscher. But when the request reached the desk of Artemus Gates, now the undersecretary of the Navy, he recommended changing the award to a Distinguished Service Medal.

In making his recommendations for the higher award, Gates praised Steichen: "Not only have his own efforts been unbelievably tireless for a man of his age, but he has inspired all those under him," Gates wrote. "I feel he has made one of the greatest single contributions of this war toward giving the people of our country a favorable and honest interpretation of the navy's role."

Most of the Steichen unit members were able to use their association with the old man to help get them restarted in civilian life.

In 1946, both George Kidder Smith and Wayne Miller received awards from the Guggenheim Foundation to continue their photography. Kidder Smith's award was to be used for photographing architectural subjects; Miller's was to be used for documenting the lives of Chicago's black urban dwellers, an idea that had come to him while he was on an aircraft carrier in the Pacific.

Miller would remain the closest to Steichen over the years, first helping him edit the massive *Family of Man* exhibit in New York. With Steichen's guidance, Miller joined Robert Capa's Magnum Agency, of which he remains a member today, even though he has long retired from active shooting.

Having spent most of his savings to support his wife through her difficulties, Charles Kerlee elected to pick up his commercial photographic career in New York instead of returning to Los Angeles, where he had lived before the war. The move quickly reestablished him in the advertising world as a leading commercial illustrator.

Marty Forscher, who had taught himself camera repair in the unit's lab and quickly garnered a reputation for being able to fix seemingly unrepairable cameras, also set up shop in New York, and quickly became the biggest name in camera repair in America.

Barrett Gallagher and his wife freelanced in Africa for two years before moving back to New York. Gallagher then began to draw regular assignments from *Fortune*. He would continue his relationship with now-full-admiral Gerald Bogan. This access helped him cover Navy operations for the next two decades, documenting the coming of the nuclear age and the evolution of naval aviation. His 1950s book *Flattop* went through a number of revisions and printings.

Two ships, the building of which Gallagher covered in the early 1960s, remain in service today. The aircraft carriers *Kitty Hawk* and *Enterprise* remain the longest serving ships in the U.S. Navy; *Kitty* will decommission in early 2009, while *Enterprise* is scheduled to leave service in 2012.

While they were in New York wrapping up their Navy business before being released from active duty, Jacobs, Jorgensen, and Bristol conceived the most ambitious postwar scheme of the unit members.

According to the December 1945 issue of *Fortune,* they marched into the magazine's New York offices "still wearing the naval officers' uniforms and the ribbons they won serving with Captain Edward Steichen's camera unit." Their scheme: "to divide the world into three parts, each to be covered for a year and a half by one of them."

The magazine's editors agreed to give it a shot and guaranteed them enough money to get started. Bristol, who had dreamed up the three-way plan, chose to cover Asia; Jorgensen selected Africa; Jacobs headed for Europe.

Steichen, meanwhile, still felt he was too young to retire and accepted a position as the photographic director at New York's Museum of Modern Art, the scene of his two successful shows. He remained active with the Navy and was often invited back to speak at Navy occasions. He even returned to active duty for three weeks in 1950 in order to tour Navy photographic facilities in the Pacific and recommend changes.

An effort to get Steichen promoted to rear admiral on the retired list was made in the 1950s. Some members of Congress planned to put forth legislation, required by law to advance anyone on the Navy's retired list, but in the end, the plan failed. The Navy refused to go along with the promotion, stating that Steichen's Distinguished Service Medal had been sufficient reward for his contributions.

New York City celebrating the surrender of Japan. They threw anything and kissed anybody in Times Square, August 14, 1945.

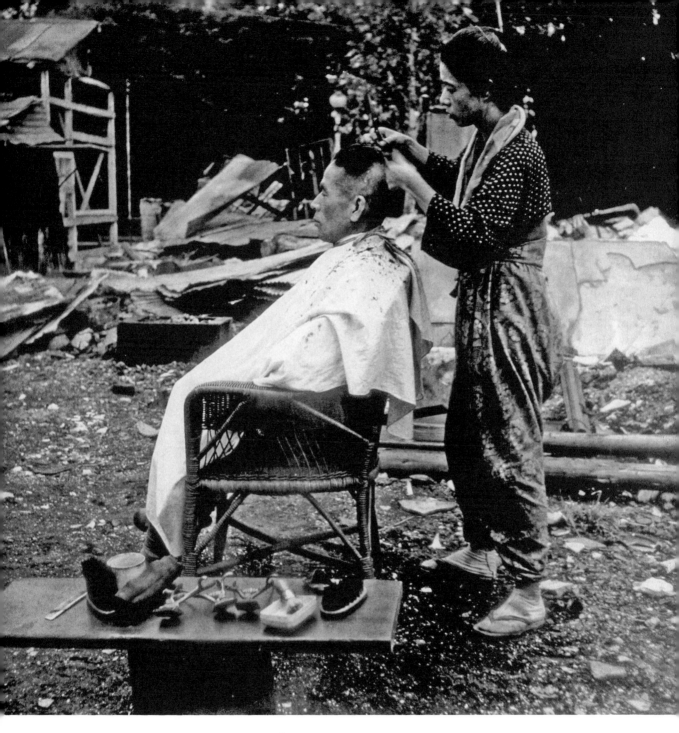

A Japanese civilian gets a haircut amid the rubble of Yokohama, Japan.

ABOVE: *Wounded soldiers, sailors, and Marines watch a movie featuring Betty Grable on board the hospital ship*
Solace *off Okinawa.*

OPPOSITE: *A sailor on board the destroyer* Jarvis *works during a*
combat drill while at sea in the South Pacific in February 1945.

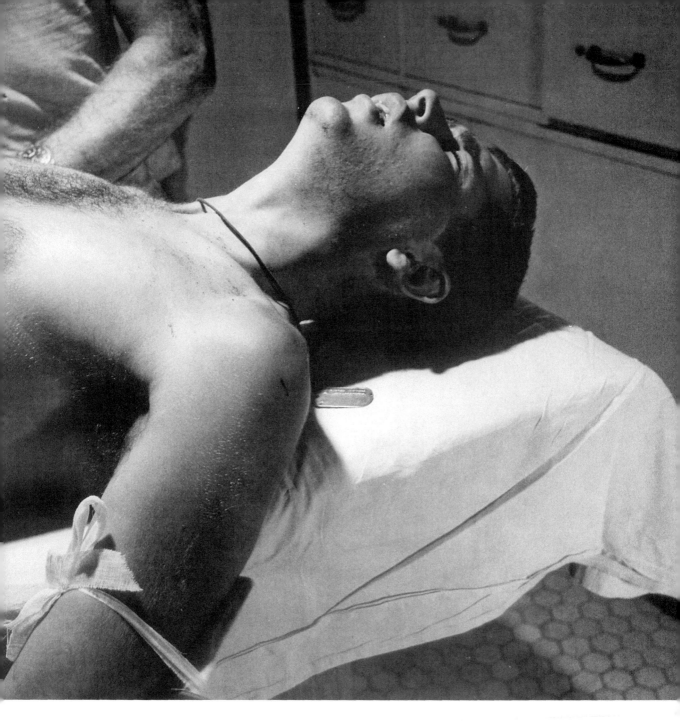

Private First Class A. Check lies on an operating table on the hospital ship Solace *off the Okinawa coast.*

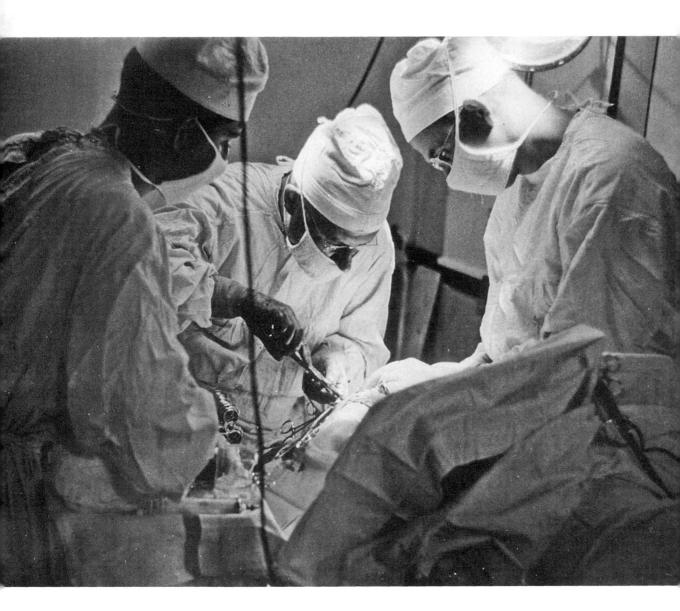

Emergency surgery being performed on a wounded soldier on board the hospital ship Solace *off Okinawa.*

Aboard the USS Kitty Hawk, *June 5, 2008, Aviation Boatswain's Mate Third Class Thomas Burress of V-2 Division signals that all is clear as an F/A-18 Hornet leaves the waist catapults during flight operations in the Western Pacific.*

THE NAVY AND STEICHEN'S LEGACY

✦ ✦ ✦

A S I REACH the end of writing this book in the summer of 2008, I am on board the aircraft carrier *Kitty Hawk* passing through areas of the Pacific that seem haunted by memories of Steichen's men. Tokyo Bay, Guam, Wake Island, and eventually Pearl Harbor pass before my eyes and the eyes of the ship's crew.

This mighty ship herself will soon become a part of history, as she is on her way back to the United States to be taken out of service—the last conventional carrier in the Navy's active inventory of ships.

Not only am I moving on the same waters as Steichen's men, I am doing basically the same job—trying to tell the stories of a ship and her crew.

The legacy of Steichen is still with the Navy today. In 1963, the service, seeking the kind of communicators they'd had in the Steichen unit, started a photojournalism program at Syracuse University where sailors could go and study the crafts of writing, photography, and graphics.

This yearlong program takes promising writers and photographers from the Navy's enlisted ranks and turns them into professionals. Many have left the Navy and gone on to careers in the private sector. Others had made the Navy a career.

I was fortunate to attend the course in 1983 as a young Navy second-class photographer's mate. Now, nearly forty-five years after its creation, the program has adapted to the digital age and is still producing excellent communicators.

But the Navy's culture has changed just enough these days to allow enlisted sailors the same freedom of movement to cover Navy operations that it granted to Steichen's officers.

June 21, 2008: A deck seaman stands lookout watch as the aircraft carrier Kitty Hawk *steams close enough to Wake Island for sailors to get a glimpse of the "Alamo of the Pacific," where U.S. Marines made a heroic stand in December 1941. This photo was taken at the approximate position as Steichen unit photographer Charles Kerlee's famous photo of Wake Island burning in the background and a fighter aircraft silhouetted in the foreground.*

June 10, 2008: Aerial views of the aircraft carrier Kitty Hawk *operating in the Western Pacific.*

Aboard the USS Kitty Hawk, *June 25, 2008, Machinist's Mate First Class (SW) Damien Kelly, leading petty officer for 1 Main Machinery Room, makes rounds in his main space, looking for problems.*

Steichen always remembered his tie to the Navy fondly and occasionally used his Navy captain's title in retirement. Though he received no pension, as he had not completed the required years of service to merit this, Steichen was still entitled to the trappings and title his position offered.

In 1963, at the twenty-year anniversary of the Navy Photographic Center at Naval Station Anacostia in Washington, D.C., Steichen, then in his eighties, addressed the crowd: "I am extremely fond of the Navy and of my time on active duty," he told them. "I am especially fond of one thing the service has given me."

Pointing to the black tie he was wearing, Steichen went on to say that he had grown fond of black ties and "had worn nothing other than a Navy black tie" since he had left active service.

So in the end, it wasn't just Steichen who had left his mark on the Navy. The Navy, too, had left its mark on Steichen.

FOLLOWING PAGE: *Aboard the USS* Kitty Hawk, *June 25, 2008, aviation machinist's mates test an F/A-18 jet engine on the ship's fantail before clearing the engine fit to be reinstalled in an aircraft.*

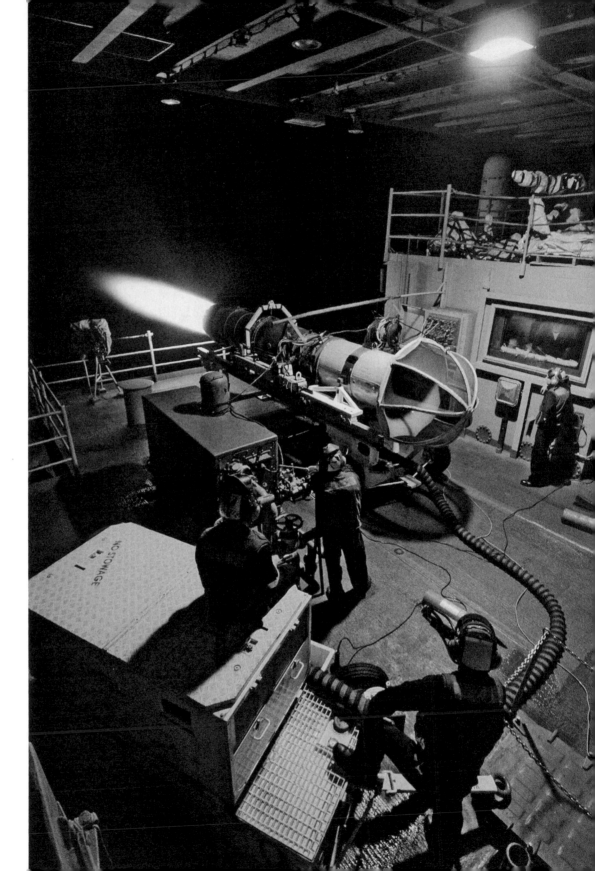

PHOTO CREDITS

Commodore M. C. Perry, Narative of the Expedition to China Seas and Japan, 1852–1854, U.S. Government. Eliphalet M. Brown, National Archives: pages 5, 6, 7, and 8.

Lieutenant Victor Jorgensen: pages 10, 13, 167, 168-169, 170, 204, 206, 216, 218, 219, 220, and 221.

Edward Steichen, courtesy George Eastman House: pages 17, 21, and 22.

U.S. Navy photo in the collection of the National Archives: pages 19, 20, 23, 25, 27, 28, 31, 32, 35, 37, 39, 41, 42, 45, 48, 49, 52, 58, 61, 62, 63, 81, 96, 114, 150, 153, 155, 197, 199, 207, and 208.

Lieutenant Horace Bristol: pages 66, 72–73, 82, 83, 84–85, 86, 87, 89, 90, 91, 139, 149, and 195 (top).

Captain Edward Steichen: pages 71, 76, 93, 95, 123, 126, 131, 133, 134, 148, and 200–201.

Lieutenant Charles Fenno Jacobs: pages 78, 79, 94, 97, 102, 105, 136, 137, 164, 171, 172, 174, 175, 176, 177, 178, 182, 183, 184, 185, 186, 187, 188, 189, and 196 (bottom).

Lieutenant Charles Kerlee: pages 88, 92, 107, 110–111, 113, 118, 140, 141, 142, 195 (bottom), 196 (top), and 199.

Lieutenant Wayne F. Miller: pages 98, 115, 117, 121, 122, 124, 125, 128, 129, 143, 144, 145, 146, 147, 179, 180, 190, 192, 203, 209, 210, 211, 212, and 217.

Specialist (P) First Class Alfonso Iannelli: page 106.

Ensign Thomas Binford: pages 156, 159, and 162.

Lieutenant Barrett Gallagher: pages 181, 191, and 213.

Photographer's Mate Second Class Raymond Smith: page 198

Mark D. Faram: pages 222, 224, 225, and 226.

BIBLIOGRAPHY

✯   ✯   ✯

Bachner, Evan. *At Ease: Navy Men of World War II*. New York: Harry N. Abrams, 2004.

Bristol, Horace. *Japan: 14 Volume Set*. Tokyo, Japan: East-West at Toppan Press, 1949.

————. *Tokyo on a Five-Day Pass with Candid Camera*. Tokyo, Japan: Toppan Press, 1951.

Gallagher, Barrett. *Flattop: The Action-Packed Story of U.S. Aircraft Carriers, Past and Present*. New York: Doubleday, 1959.

Kerlee, Charles. *Pictures with a Purpose—How They Are Made*. San Francisco: Camera Craft Publishing Company, 1939.

Miller, Max. *Daybreak for Our Carrier*. New York: Whittlesey House, 1944.

————. *It's Tomorrow Out Here*. New York: Whittlesey House, 1945.

————. *The Far Shore*. New York: Whittlesey House, 1945.

Niven, Penelope. *Steichen: A Biography*. New York: Random House, 1997.

Phillips, Christopher. *Steichen at War*. New York: Harry N. Abrams Co., 1981

————. *Steichen*. Degree thesis, 1979.

Steichen, Edward. *A Life in Photography*. New York: Doubleday, 1963.

————. *Power in the Pacific: A Pictorial Record of Navy Combat Operations on Land, Sea and in the Sky*. New York: U.S. Camera Publishing Company, 1945.

————. *The Blue Ghost: A Photographic Log and Personal Narrative of the Aircraft Carrier USS Lexington in Combat Operations*. New York: Harcourt Brace, 1947.

The Road to Victory. Metropolitan Museum of Modern Art. New York, 1941.

Warren, Mame. Unpublished interviews with Marion Warren, 1987.

INDEX